Solomon Brenner

BLACK BELT PARENTING

with Rochelle Brenner

*The Art Of Raising
Children For "Success"*

Foreword By
Omar Periu

Shark Publishing
Feasterville, PA 19053

ISBN 0-974-63080-2

Manufactured in the United States of America
10 09 08 07 06

Table of Contents

Dedication

Acknowledgements

Foreword

Introduction

To my Mom and Dad.

Your infinite love and support made me believe
I could do anything. Thank you!

ACKNOWLEDGEMENTS

I would like to thank all of the Action Karate Instructors who saw the vision and are now the driving force of empowerment for their students.

Another thank you goes to my sister Rochelle Brenner – a great journalist, for help writing and significant guidance.

Thanks also to Dan and Mary Baldwin who provided the editorial guidance for Black Belt Parenting.

Thank you Mr. Omar Periu for your constant guidance.

Thank you to Michael Dalzell, a student and friend, for your editorial contribution.

FOREWORD

by
Omar Periu

One of the joys of my work is that I'm constantly meeting new people with new ideas and new ways of looking at the world around us. One of those good people is Solomon Brenner. Getting to know him and being in a position to hear his unique perspective on life has been a real bonus for me.

Now, through <u>Black Belt Parenting</u> you can get to know this remarkable young man. More important, you can read, understand and put to good use his remarkable concepts for raising kids. Solomon cares about kids and he realizes that the future of the nation will someday be in their hands. One of his lifelong goals is to help make those hands as capable as possible.

Placing his proven techniques into the hands of the nation's parents is one of the many ways he is contributing to a better society.

Behind his advice, you will find an attitude and it's a sound one. Solomon believes that you can't have good kids without parents *who know how to be good parents.* This is your guidebook and your inspiration for becoming good parents.

Solomon uses the ancient techniques of karate to build sound bodies, good minds, discipline, respect, courtesy, responsibility and dignity in children and young adults. These same techniques can and should be taken beyond the gym and into the home. <u>Black Belt Parenting</u> shows you how to do just that.

Karate and parenting are ancient and noble skills. Solomon Brenner has seen them in a new light, creating a new way to grow great kids. This is a remarkable book. Enjoy it. Put it to work. And we will all enjoy the benefits.

Omar Periu

INTRODUCTION

I have been instructing children in karate for more than nine years and I have learned much from teaching martial arts. A lot of that learning involves parents and parenting. I've often had to correct, discipline or motivate children and I've made plenty of mistakes in doing so. Karate is an excellent learning tool for teacher as well as student. I would like to share what I've learned to help you when you need to correct, discipline or motivate your children.

My view is almost that of a spectator watching a movie or reading a book. In those situations you know exactly what you would do or what the character should do. You are removed from the situation and look at it from a distance. It's not that you don't care, it's just that you see the situation objectively. The characters' errors are obvious. Looking back now, I see the errors I and many parents have made.

Making mistakes is not bad parenting. Like anything else, it's a way to grow and learn. I've seen parents make decisions for their children that I knew could turn out disastrously. I also knew that those parents made that decision believing whole heartedly that it was the best thing for the child. Good parenting makes you totally involved so each and every decision is made with emotion, especially love. Logic is not always involved and this can cause turmoil for parents because all you ever want is the very best for your child.

My story begins in 1994 when I opened my first martial arts school, Action Karate. I was only 20 years old. I had been teaching for a few years and thought I knew a lot. What did I know about business or teaching children? I didn't know much about either, but I did know karate. My partner Jacqueline and I wanted to have the best karate school around. We wanted lots of students. We wanted to be number one: the most confident, disciplined and physically elite. And we worked day and night to market our business, enroll the new students, teach the classes, clean the school, and work other jobs to pay the bills and go to college full time. It was a good thing we were young, because we really needed that energy to keep up our strict schedule with enthusiasm.

I really began to love teaching. And I thought I was great at it. I especially liked teaching the children who were just like little soldiers. There were a few of them who were always put together just right: not a hair out of place, uniforms always neat and ironed, and the belt never falling off. They were happy to come to class and excited to "yes sir" and "no sir" me with just the right amount of enthusiasm. They were the "A" students. You knew they were going to show up for class on time and you could count on them to lead everybody else.

We were getting lots of "A" students, so many that we took the best of the "A"s and created a special team for them, the demo team. They would travel to local venues and camps demonstrating the martial arts talents and the skills necessary to earn a black belt. One rule for being appointed to the demo team was to have dedication and commitment to earning your black belt. They were required to join a special program called the black belt course. The course was for students who knew without a doubt, they would never quit. Nothing would get in the way of achieving that goal. Their parents approved a special permission slip so that everyone knew this was a serious commitment. One boy in particular, John, was training in the black belt training course and was invited to join the demo team. He showed up for all of his practices and trained as hard as he could. He was really advancing through the system and we knew for sure that John would be one of the greatest Black Belts that our school ever produced.

Then it happened - John quit and it felt like a knife through my heart! It was getting too hard for him and he wanted to stay home and play with his friends. I was sure that this was a temporary set back, common to most children at one point or another. I believed his parents would talk to him about commitment and the importance of completing set goals and bring him back to class the next week. Boy was I wrong. His parents thought it was crazy to make their child do anything that he didn't want to do. And he was only 6 months from earning his black belt. I knew in my heart that those parents were making a mistake. Allowing Johnny to quit would set the precedent for a lifetime of quitting. John was an "A" student. Just imagine what can happen to the "B" and "C" students.

The day John quit was the day I realized that *parents need the lessons as much as the children.* I felt like I had failed as a teacher and as a motivator, not just to John, but to his family and his future. I made a decision to read as much as I could on parenting and motivation and attend as many seminars on the subject as possible. I had to become an expert on the subject of parenting and combine that with the discipline of karate if I was ever going to get kids *and their parents* to the black belt level.

Our school did well, we graduated hundreds of black belts. What happened between 1994 and today? A lot! I learned a lot about motivating children and about motivating adults. My goal in this book is to share with others the fun and frenzy about kids, about how to correct, discipline and motivate them and how to keep it all positive.

This book is about getting parents to the black belt level.

Chapter 1

Challenging To Be The Best

"It's lack of faith that makes people afraid of meeting challenges, and I believed in myself."
                                                        Muhammad Ali

There are no problems to be solved. There are only challenges to be met. Raising children is both a challenge and opportunity. For most parents, it is the most challenging task in their lives and the one that can afford the most rewards and heart-wrenching disappointments. Raising children is an opportunity to cast your love, light and knowledge to others, to help them grow into the people you know they can be so they can achieve their greatest potential.

Your children have faults. Sometimes they will break the rules, and how you respond to those infractions will have a lasting impact on their development.

"We who have the final word can speak softly or angrily. We can seek to challenge and annoy, as we need not stay docile and quiet."
                                                        William O Douglas
                                    Associate Justice of the US Supreme Court

Douglas was speaking about a judicial decision when he said this, but his words also speak to the role of parents. Parents have the job of challenging their children even if it means annoying them. As a karate instructor, I use that philosophy in class.

Black Belt Parenting

Challenging your children will introduce them to the concept of "cause and effect." When the bedroom is clean (cause), there's time for an extra hour of TV (effect). When the green beans are eaten, cake is an option for dessert. When a child misbehaves, the effect should be a learned lesson, not a prolonged punishment. The effect will determine if and how they learn from the situation. The philosophies in <u>Black Belt Parenting</u> will help you create a positive effect from such efforts so there is genuine, positive and long-term learning.

When I started teaching, my standard procedure was to condemn children who did not satisfy my expectations or execute their moves perfectly. I would use punishments such as making students do push-ups in front of the class or run laps. I thought that by pointing out their flaws, they would focus their efforts on fixing them.

That was my flaw.

Pointing out their flaws did not motivate anyone to fix anything. I just created a negative focus on the situation. If the students couldn't immediately meet expectations, they would become frustrated and not want to continue training. The students who practiced the least got the most attention. It became clear that the only way a student could get attention was by messing up. My focus on flaws was the cause that resulted in the effect of students seeking negative attention.

I learned about the concept of challenging at a seminar in

Florida. The speaker said, "Instead of criticizing your employees, challenge them. Instead of insulting someone for a blunder, challenge him or her to improve their methods of doing things. Instead of being complacent where you are, challenge yourself to improve your life and the lives of people around you."

Those are great goals and a worthwhile way of looking at situations. I incorporated challenging in class and encouraged parents to do the same. It worked so well that I have enough success stories to fill an entire book!

Instead of focusing on the errors, I learned how to focus on what's right and use that as a launching pad to suggest potential improvements. It worked great! Enrollment increased, retention rate increased and I have a much better relationship with students and their parents.

The competition is no longer for negative attention, but for positive accomplishment.   Now the only way to get attention in class is to pay attention and do your best. Instead of doing push-ups as punishment, students compete to do the best or the most push-ups. This same, positive, martial arts approach can work just as well for you and your children.

Getting Started

The key to a successful challenge is making sure the reward is appropriate. Money and junk food can be rewards for certain situations, but positive feedback can also be a reward. In class, positive attention counts as a reward. Something as simple as a high-five can go a long way.

I posed a challenge to students in class to do something nice for their mother one Mother's Day. A few children suggested ideas. The next day I found out from the parents that they had not followed through with promises to clean up their toys and clear off the dinner table as they so proudly suggested in class.

When I gathered the class before bowing out, I asked what everyone had done for Mother's Day. Few children raised their hands and most stared at the floor. One boy, Bradley, had lived up to his word and had cleaned up his room as promised. I decided to make Bradley an example so that others would emulate his kindness.

I set up a chair on the practice floor and lifted him up to stand on it. He nervously stood about 6 feet up and smiled at the class. I directed the rest of the students to line up behind me on the other side of the gym. We ran up one by one to give Bradley running high-fives. Bradley was a positive example and the other students envied his position. Bradley smiled from ear to ear as the center of attention and laughed as students jumped to reach his outstretched hand for a high-five.

The next day before class started, I didn't even have to ask. Five children tugged on my pant legs with eager stories of helping at home and asking if they could stand on the chair, too. Parents were astonished at how the threat of punishment was not needed to motivate the children to do something good.

Anytime a student goes above and beyond what is expected or accomplishes a meaningful goal, I set up the chair and show him or her appreciation with a round of high-fives. It is a simple reward, but it works.

What version of the chair can you set up in your home?

Sometimes a challenge is necessary in response to bad behavior. In one case, a student wasn't doing his homework and his grades were steadily falling. Tony's teacher had called the house several times to let his mom know he wasn't doing his work. His mom had tried taking away his video games, his bike and allowance, but Tony still wasn't improving his schoolwork.

His mom asked for my help. "I've tried everything. I know Tony listens to you. Is there anything you can tell him to get him to do his schoolwork? Tell him he can't go to class unless he does his work," she said. I told her that it was a bad idea to threaten removing him from class, especially when karate was such a positive influence in his life. It would be like taking away the vegetables from an otherwise unhealthy meal.

Rather than threaten to take karate from Tony, I sat down and talked with him. I asked him why he wasn't doing his work and he just shrugged. Tony was not motivated and I hoped a challenge would spark his interest.

The challenge: I suggested that if he did his homework for two straight weeks without missing a single assignment, I would buy him McDonald's for lunch, bring it to him at school and eat with him. Two weeks later, guess who was treated to McDonald's? Tony met the challenge because he could see the reward – a fun, free lunch. Tony wasn't a bad kid. He just didn't feel satisfaction from doing his homework.

However, he did feel satisfaction out of meeting his challenge. His mom was delighted and started using the same system of rewards to deal with Tony.

From then on, she had a system centered on the belief that he could have anything he wanted as long as he earned it. He didn't always get McDonald's or toys; instead, his positive actions were rewarded with positive activities. For good grades, his mom would take her son to the park to shoot hoops, to the local recreation center to swim, or to extra karate classes. The system of rewards was much more effective than punishing failure. That's Black Belt Parenting!

The best reward you can give your children is spending time with them. Tony's mom gave rewards such as taking walks with him, inviting him to help cook a dinner of his choice or going to the library together. Giving time as a reward benefits parent and child. Nothing can replace the time a parent spends with their children. If you are busy, get around it by inviting your child to be part of something you have to do, such as helping cook dinner. Make it fun by making a favorite dish or dessert.

If you have work to do at home, make it possible for your child to help. For example, if you are preparing for a job interview, a speech or presentation, practice with your child. It is important to include your children in as much of your life as you can. And challenging is one of the most effective methods around.

Think Like The Rich

Challenges can give your children lessons in economics and show them how hard work (cause) earns money and prestige (effect).

Send the message that they can have anything they want as long as they work for it. Not only that, but the more they achieve in rewards the more confidence they will have, and the more successful they will feel. The more successful they feel, the more in control they will be. Successful businesspeople employ these techniques and rich people think this way. You should, too.

It is unreasonable to offer rewards out of your price range or their maturity level, but you don't have to say 'no' all the time, either. Instead of denying requests, allow them with a condition. When a child wants to stay up an hour later than bedtime, allow him or her to do it as long as half the extra time is spent doing chores. If the child wants to go to an amusement park, set up rules so that when the family loads into the car, the child feels a sense of victory and accomplishment. *I did this,* they will think. *I earned this.*

The economics lessons weren't missed by an 8-year-old student, Jason, who wanted to buy a video featuring his favorite television characters. Jason's mother agreed to buy him the video as long as he put his toys away every day for a month without being asked. If he had to be asked, he would start over from "day one." Needless to say, Jason had his video a month later and continued to put his toys away because it became a positive and rewarded activity. He would not have developed the habit without first being offered a reward.

For his next request, Jason wanted to buy nunchakus. These are wooden sticks held together by chains and are used in karate as a weapon and teaching tool. Jason was a model student at karate and earned straight A's in school. However, nunchakus were still not appropriate for his age. Jason's mother and I agreed that his hands were not big enough and he lacked the coordination to control nunchakus. Jason could hurt himself or someone else trying to master them. Even professional martial artists occasionally slip and injure themselves or a training partner with them.

As a compromise, Jason's mother told him that if he continued to meet the challenge of earning straight A's, he could have rubber nunchakus. Once he mastered those, he could have the wooden ones. Jason agreed, thinking he would have his adult "chucks" in a matter of weeks. Jason was excited and eager to move on to the next level so he practiced often. Still, nunchakus are a very challenging tool and he didn't move on to adult chucks until he was 13.

Age-appropriate rewarding applies to older children as well.
A 14-year-old student, Aaron, wanted an off-road three-wheeler
bike and nothing else. However, his parents rightfully said he
could not have one because he was legally too young and
three-wheelers are expensive and potentially dangerous vehicles.

Aaron was indignant and insisted that because he got good
grades, he should get the reward he wanted. The appropriate
response in such a case is to compromise, or suggest he can
have a three-wheeler when he earns enough money to buy it
himself. That scenario eliminates the chance Aaron will be riding
an ATV before his 16th birthday because it will take so long to
raise the money.

It is not necessary to give in to every reward your child
wants. Even as you are raising your child in a positive atmosphere, it is important to maintain the role of disciplinarian
because children are your responsibility. Even as parents fulfill
their role as disciplinarians there are ways to make the positive
messages stick. One way to challenge is to use competition.
There are many activities that can incorporate competition and
in most cases the child won't even realize it is a challenge.

Use a timer. In class, students told to do 20 laps grudgingly
jogged around the practice floor. When I started using a timer
to challenge them, students pushed themselves to beat their old
times. By putting a time limit on the exercise, students used the

challenge to put some wind under their heels. This can also be applied at home. Students can be timed to clean their room, wash the dishes, or do any chores. Try it. I believe you will be happy with your results.

Mixed Messages: Don't Punish with "Positivity"

Many karate schools still use push-ups as punishment for students who misbehave. As this becomes a routine punishment, it doesn't take long before push-ups are the most dreaded activity. But they're a great exercise. Now I offer the opportunity to do push-ups as a way to get better, not a punishment for failure. When I abandoned them as punishment and embraced them as rewards, students changed their attitude as well.

When someone isn't paying attention in class, I don't demand push-ups. I try to make them want to change their behavior by challenging them.

A student named Teddy was a troublemaker and his lack of attention distracted other students as well. He would do the wrong exercise or make funny noises. I tried to ignore him, but had reached the end of my rope when he was imitating Power Rangers while he did the moves.

I felt insulted that this student was making a mockery of my class. I worked very hard to keep everyone's attention and I knew that he was trying to challenge me. It is a feeling that parents echo when they find their children won't listen. I decided to make an example of Teddy and loudly pointed out his flaws.

"Why are you making those noises?" I asked sternly, "Let's see what happens when you hold your arms out for the rest of the class, if you're still making noises."

Teddy was embarrassed and resentful. His ego was as sore as his arms. As soon as his punishment time was over, he went right back to his previous attitude. I was livid. But the next day I employed a different strategy – challenging him – and it worked wonders on Teddy's attitude.

Although I was tempted to yell at Teddy the next time I noticed him drifting off, I asked him to demonstrate a particular kick in front of the class. I chose an easy one because I didn't want to embarrass him. Teddy kicked as high as he could, but his energy was low. I asked him to lead the class in doing 10 kicks. Now everyone was looking at Teddy as a leader, and it was time for him to measure up. He mustered his energy and directed the class through 10 kicks. Every time he kicked, it was the best I'd ever seen him do. Each one was better than the last. He loudly directed the class through the kicks like a confident teacher. He was poised in front of the class with a look of determination on his face.

When Teddy returned to his place in line, he paid close attention and practiced with intensity as if everybody was still looking at him as a leader. His confidence was up and he didn't think about making jokes for attention anymore. If he were called on again to be a leader, he wanted to impress the class by setting a good example. Teddy realized that if he was going to be an example to others, he had to keep improving so the others were impressed with his skill.

Lou Holtz, the legendary Notre Dame football coach, said, "How you respond to the challenge in the second half will determine what you become after the game, whether you are a winner or a loser." In the first half, I was losing to Teddy because I couldn't control my anger. In the second half, I tried a different strategy and Teddy and I both became winners.

Push-ups and similar exercises are an opportunity to show off and build strength, rather than induce humiliation. Children could also be encouraged to do simple, repetitive exercises at home as a reward. Doing homework and reading should not be viewed as punishment, either. Children should think of them as events that create a positive reward.

In another class, the problem was not a lack of trying. The student was trying and still failing. As we practiced a technique over and over, 10-year old Caroline was the only person who kept using the wrong hand, stepping the wrong way or forgetting a step. The rest of the class was ready to move on, but she was stuck and I had to keep calling her name to instruct her to switch her feet, step the other way or turn around. I did not insult her, but it was clear that Caroline didn't think she could cut it. A few other students noticed her struggling and she was getting embarrassed.

Instead of giving up on her for falling behind, I remembered to try the system of challenging. I did not want Caroline to give up, so I told her a story about the time I couldn't do a single push-up, but by practicing every day, I had built up my strength to do hundreds. Caroline was in a similar predicament.

In this example, part of the challenge was pointing out that perfection does not come easy and practicing is the key to reaching perfection. I told her the example of my past shortfalls to let her know that success is just around the corner. She accepted the challenge.

After hearing of examples when I didn't quite meet the grade, Caroline felt more *normal*. Since other people overcame the same kind of frustration that she went through, she resolved to keep trying. Caroline did not execute the technique in class that day, but she did show an abundance of determination. Nearly a week later, Caroline finally nailed her technique. She came to class a few minutes early and demonstrated her accomplishment.

"Mr. B, look! I can do it now!" she said. With that kind of confidence, Caroline was eager to be first in line for the next technique.

If you can't say something nice, don't say anything at all. That philosophy works in karate class and it will work in the home. Before pointing out flaws, find something positive to say. I would never say, "You're doing that kick wrong and you haven't been able to do it right once all day. Give me 10 push-ups. Don't show me those sissy kicks again tomorrow."

I choose a specific aspect of the kick and challenge the student to meet the goal. For example, "That was a great effort. This time, point your toes and snap the kick." The student needs direction and specific advice for improvement. If a student isn't punching the target correctly, I say, "Those are such strong punches. Try not to bend your wrist and strike with this part of your hand so that you don't break your wrist."

The same method can be used in almost any situation to challenge your children.

If your children have trouble with a homework assignment, patiently go over it with them. If he or she worked hard on a model airplane and some of the pieces are in the wrong place, do not point out the flaws. Instead, point out the good work by carefully gluing the pieces together and sticking to the project. After the child has confidence, offer to help build the next model airplane and show how to follow the instructions.

With Energy To Spare

Asking a child to stop running around rarely works. Children have more energy than adults and don't have the patience to store it for later. Rather than yelling or insisting on a certain mode of behavior, find an activity that distracts them from causing problems.

I was in a medical waiting room where another patient had a

three-year-old child wearing out the patience of everyone in the office. The mother occasionally smiled apologetically but it did nothing to appease the crowded room of sniffling, aching, coughing visitors. To make matters worse, the young girl had just eaten a lollipop. As she darted around the room, she left a trail of sticky handprints on chairs and the pants of some visitors.

One older lady could not hold back her anger and said, "Excuse me, please control your child. She is running around here out of control and making a mess. I am annoyed and the rest of this waiting room is annoyed and you aren't doing anything about it."

The woman was hurt and offended to hear those words. I could see that it felt like that woman slapped her with the accusation that she wasn't a fit mother. As she tried to hold back tears, the mother desperately attempted to control her daughter, but the quick toddler would squirm away. "Damn it, sit still!" she shouted in a desperate attempt to show the angry old woman she was trying. The startled little girl sat still for a few minutes then returned to playing around the room.

A very bright woman in the waiting room suggested the mother play a game that might distract the little girl. No one had any games and there wasn't enough room to set up any physical activities. Since the mom didn't understand her options, the woman began to engage the young girl in conversation.

She began a story of a fairly tale princess living in a faraway land. She allowed the girl to fill in details of the story and they developed the plot together. The girl was so busy trying to think of an outrageous way to slay the dragon, the others in the waiting room barely even noticed her. By engaging the girl's mind and interests, the woman succeeded in changing the girl's behavior. The girl had been running around because she had nothing better to do and merely "sitting still" was not an intriguing way to spend her time.

Another option is to give the child a pen and a piece of paper to draw a picture of a house or brontosaurus or their favorite foods. That is a constructive use of time and it avoids an embarrassing situation in which the child is running around and, in this case, disturbing other patients and medical personnel.

There is no situation that justifies using angry words to judge your child's performance. "Damn it, sit still" is unacceptable behavior from an adult.

Abraham Lincoln found a way to compliment a general who had put Union troops in danger during the dark days of the Civil War and had even insulted his president's leadership abilities. It's a wonderful expression of how to use words to make your point even in a tense and difficult situation. I first read this story in How To Win Friends And Influence People by Dale Carnegie.

General Joseph Hooker, head of the Army of the Potomac, was the offending party. Lincoln was facing scrutiny from the public and Congress while his men were dying. Each battle was a struggle for survival of the Union. Even facing these odds, Lincoln tactfully used a challenge to motivate the general rather than berate him for his blunders.

In a famous letter to Hooker written April 26, 1863, Lincoln wrote, " ... I think it best for you to know that there are some things in regard to which I am not quite satisfied with you." Lincoln went on, "You are ambitious, which, within reasonable bounds, does good rather than harm. But I think that during General Burnside's command of the army you have taken counsel of your ambition and thwarted him as much as you could, in which you did a great wrong to the country and to a most meritorious and honorable brother officer."

Lincoln does a wonderful job of citing the positive, then explaining the criticism. Lincoln concludes his letter with the statement, "Beware of rashness, but with energy and sleepless vigilance go forward and give us victories."

And when children challenge your ability to challenge them, hold steady and don't let them intimidate you. In the words of former CBS commentator Elmer Davis, "The first and great commandment is, don't let them scare you." In parenting, the stakes and emotional toll are high. Children can be unpredictable and try to flex their rebellion in ways you're not prepared for, but don't let them scare you. Maintain your authority.

Introducing the concept of challenges in how you handle your children may help prevent adverse situations in the future, or at least ensure that your child will learn from mistakes.

Learn a lesson from Muhammad Ali. Have faith, meet your challenges in life, and believe in yourself—essential steps in mastering the art of Black Belt Parenting.

Chapter 2

Do Not "Don't!"

"We must not ignore the small daily differences we can make which, over time, add up to big differences that we often cannot foresee."

Marian Wright Edelman
Founder and President of the
Children's Defense Fund

Here's the scenario: you are talking on the phone and your son is laughing so loud with one of his pals that you can barely hear yourself talking, let alone your friend. What do you say?

a) "Don't be so loud."

b) "Speak quietly."

There may not appear to be a big difference between "Don't be so loud" and "Speak quietly." Both might accomplish the same goal—the child will lower the volume of his voice. However, using the word "don't" puts a negative slant to the comment. Something as simple as taking the word "don't" out of your vocabulary can make a huge difference in how a child reacts to your words.

Your child will probably tone down his voice with either response. When you say, "Don't be so loud," he thinks about how he has a loud voice and the words "so loud" resonate in his head. If the response is a more positive "Speak quietly," he merely thinks about changing the volume of his voice to a lower level.

Even though "Don't be so loud" may have the same effect as "Speak quietly" in the short-term, the overall benefit of using positive words can have an impact on your child's future self-esteem and behavior. Negative words send the message that the child was doing something wrong. Positive words turn the message into a request. "Don't" draws attention to the flaw so that the child can not think of anything else.

There is a humorous story of a father I know, Mr. Krane, who learned a lesson about using "Don't" from his son, K.J. One day, they were visiting at the house of a friend. While the adults enjoyed coffee and watched golf on television, K.J. played with the friend's son of the same age. While K.J. was playing with toy cars on the floor, he accidentally cut himself. He started crying and ran to his father.

Mr. Krane saw that it was only a small cut and he asked his friend for an adhesive bandage. He gave it to his son and resumed his conversation with his friend. The kids used the buddy system to get the Band-Aid on and then K.J. dropped the wrapping on the floor.

"Don't leave that on the floor!" said Mr. Krane.

K.J. picked it up in his sore hand and continued playing. What do you think happened to the bandage wrapper? Since Dad didn't tell him what to do with it, K.J. didn't know where to put it. They were at a friend's house and he didn't want to wander around on his own or ask his friend what to do, so he just held it. Mr. Krane noticed his son was playing with one clenched fist, but he assumed it was because the bandage was a little uncomfortable. About two hours later, the Kranes were getting ready to drive home. When K.J. put on his coat, he put his hand through the sleeve and opened it just enough to reveal the wrapper. Mr. Krane and his friend started to laugh.

"Did you have that in your hand the whole time?" Mr. Krane asked.

"Yes. You told me not to put it on the floor," said K.J.

"Sure, but you could have thrown it in the trash."

K.J. was embarrassed, but Mr. Krane learned a valuable lesson. Telling his son what *not* to do just isn't good enough. In giving directions, it's better to explain what *to* do. I learned this lesson the hard way.

As part of the daily routine, I've always gathered my karate students after class to tell them announcements about upcoming events and then bow out. I kneel on the mat, and the students crowd in around me. At first, students would run into each other, push each other and fall down trying to get in place.

I would say, "Everybody come over here. Don't run." But the students did not listen. They would run anyway to get in the seats closest to me. I felt like I was losing control. The attitude during class is that students should be energetic and volunteer to display their moves, but unorganized running is not permitted at the end of class.

I started brainstorming about ways I could persuade the class to slow down for that part of the session. I finally realized I just had to rephrase the message in a positive manner. Instead of saying "Don't run," I started saying "Everybody walk over here." Most people know that when you say "don't run," you mean "walk." However, children need direct instructions. Say exactly what you want them to do, not what you don't want them to do.

There is an experiment you can try at home and on your friends to make this point. Tell your spouse or friends to look around the room, but don't look at anything red. Then tell them to close their eyes and ask, "What was blue?"

They probably won't remember because you had them concentrating on not looking at red. They won't see the blue, because they won't be looking for it. By calling attention to the color red, you immediately notice it is there. By calling attention to students running across the mat, they immediately become aware of their speed and begin racing each other. In their minds "Don't run" becomes "run!" By directing them to the act of walking, the thought of running does not even cross their minds.

This lesson is also valuable in teaching your children why it's important to look for the good in people. If I tell you to only look for blue, your recall of blue items will likely be sharp. If you only look for the bad in people, you're certain to find it. It's your decision on how to see the world.

Let's do a quick experiment to help put into perspective why someone concentrates on the words that follow "Don't." Bear with me and you will see how this applies to Black Belt Parenting.

Use your imagination to visualize a warm sunny day with a stiff breeze at your back. The sun is high and the sky is cloudless.

Don't think about the looming dark gray sky dragging storm clouds over your head. Think about the sun. Don't think about the sudden change to gloomy weather.

Don't think about the first few drops of rain smacking the sidewalk. Keep thinking about the sun. Don't think about the leak in the ceiling dripping cold water onto your cheek. Don't think about the pouring rain.

Concentrate on the bright sun that shone just a few minutes ago.

Don't think about going outside in the chilly storm wearing a T-shirt and sweatpants. Think about a blue cloudless sky.

Don't imagine yourself pulling a hood over your head as a rain shield only to splash some water collected in the hood onto your face.

Don't think about the water seeping under your jacket and into your clothes. Don't think about your chills as the frigid water slides down your neck and back.

Was it hard to concentrate on the sun shining while your imagination had droplets of rain hitting you? That's what happens when you use the word don't. It's hard to see the positive when there are negative words surrounding it.

Children who hear "don't" are being encouraged to be passive with a stifled sense of curiosity.

"Do your children view themselves as successes or failures? Are they being encouraged to be inquisitive or passive? Are they afraid to challenge authority and to question assumptions? Do they feel comfortable adapting to change? Are they easily discouraged if they cannot arrive at a solution to a problem?" wrote Lawrence Kutner, a child psychologist and author.

The right answers to those questions determine whether your child is getting a good education. Your child's education and attitude toward it starts at home.

It is important to cultivate your children's curiosity even when they are doing things they shouldn't. It would be a dreary world if children did not get their hands dirty, feet muddy or clothes creased. Help them keep their sense of adventure and love of life by telling them better things to do. Use a bit of Black Belt Parenting. Give them positive direction rather than simply saying, "Don't."

Jumping Too High

When children are not paying attention in karate class, it is necessary to work for their attention rather than punish the action with quick commands.

When Maryanne was in the beginner class, she would randomly add jumps and spins to the simple kicks I was teaching. She hadn't mastered the basic kicks and was not following along with the class. Even though I admired her efforts to attempt advanced kicks, it was disruptive during class. I did not want to discourage her from testing her limits and wanted to see her continue practicing those moves in the future.

In the past, though, I might have said, "Don't jump. Just kick," or "Turn around, stay on the ground and kick. You're not ready for those other moves."

One day in class, I walked over to Maryanne right after she had done a spinning kick and told her she had done a super powerful kick. "I hope you'll practice that at home and then it will impress everyone in the advanced class. For now, though, I'd like to see you snap a perfect simple front kick. Your spin kicks will only get better if you practice the basic moves first. I always practice simple moves before getting into the more high-flying moves."

Maryanne didn't even realize that she was being told to stop doing something she wasn't supposed to do. She saw it as a big compliment and began practicing at home. She practiced the basic kicks in class because I told her to and she believed it would help her ultimate goal. And it did!

Several times after that, she would try to catch my attention before class and show me how high her jump kicks had become. They were incredible. I also made a special effort to point out her improvement in the basic kicks so that she would get satisfaction out of practicing them as well.

Sometimes I would even practice the spin kicks with her after class so she felt like we were training together and to reward her for paying attention in class.

In another situation, I found a way to encourage students to spar without fighting. Sparring is the part of karate when students can test their skills and gain experience in a self defense situation without actually being in danger. In our school, students are required to wear protective gear on their head, mouth, hands, feet and shins. That way they can feel free to throw punches but the recipient will not be hurt.

One day I saw two advanced students, Rob and Brett, sparring before class. They had been sparring in class for years and decided to throw a few jabs at each other without putting on their protective gear. They knew that was against the rules. Rather than angrily screaming, "Don't do that! You know there's no sparring without gear," I held my tongue and asked them to train their hardest at a safer activity before class.

"Don't practice sparring" is not the message I wanted to send. I wanted them to spar, but properly, safely and by our rules. "Why don't you save sparring for class time? Try these exercises before class to improve your technique. Whenever I train for a tournament, I always practice like this," I said.

Rob and Brett were happy that they weren't in trouble and were eager to learn new moves. If I had used the word "don't" they might have felt insulted. They are great students and always show self-control when they spar, so I didn't want them to think I didn't trust them.

I said it was okay for them to practice together as long as they didn't get into sparring positions. After practicing new moves for a while, Rob suggested other moves they could do without actually hitting each other. Because I gave them the benefit of the doubt and allowed them to keep practicing and socializing, they wanted to follow the rules.

The Question Connection

You don't always have to provide an answer for what your child can do to replace their current activity. Approach the situation with a question.

If your child is sitting in front of the television, it is not necessary to tell them what to do. Merely put another idea in the child's head in the form of a question and let the ideas roll. Simply say, "Is there something else you could do? It's a beautiful day outside. Are there any activities you can play out there?"

The response could be, "I was hoping to play catch football. I'll see if my friends can play" or "Yeah, I can watch this TV show anytime. I'll go shoot hoops with my brother." A parent might be tempted to start with a "Don't," but holding off for a few seconds, thinking positively, and changing the comment will make a real difference.

In every situation where "don't" is about to come out of your mouth, think how the situation can be turned into a learning experience. What questions should your child think about before doing something? Encourage that thought process and the child will be thoughtful, engaging and reasonable in future discussions and decision making. In fact, coming up with alternatives to something they aren't allowed to do can be a challenge. Challenge them to think of something creative in place of a phrase using the word "don't."

Any child can respond to a challenge, although children under the age of five have a hard time with critical thinking and need more suggestions than questions. However, you should share your thought process with the child so they become as accustomed to responding to quandaries as you do.

For example, if a young child is trying to press the buttons on the television, don't just push their hand away or say "Don't do that."

"If you want to press buttons, here's a toy keyboard."

"If you want to watch TV, let's sit on the couch together and wrap a warm blanket around ourselves."

"You can press the off button here. After that, we will play with the stuffed animals."

Children at first will have a hard time thinking of the toy keyboard when the television buttons are the focus of their immediate attention. As they get older, they will learn that they can have their way even if they have to find an alternative that satisfies mom and dad, too. The alternative has to be a safe, fun activity.

Children might think of more dangerous things to do before coming up with an acceptable alternative. Working through that process is good training in trial and error. As long as you are there to point out the errors, the child will be steered on the right path.

As you choose the best option, consider what lesson your child will learn. Perhaps a game that teaches the alphabet by pressing buttons would be the best option for the child who wants to play with the television set. The chosen alternative should fall on the middle ground between what the child wants to do and what the parent wants the child to do.

If your child is climbing on a kitchen chair, it may be for the fun of climbing or a means to reach cookies or an effort to be rebellious. Talking to your child will reveal clues as to their real intended activity. If he or she was climbing for the fun of climbing, giving them a cookie won't satisfy the need. The best way to find out what someone wants is to ask.

"What are you trying to do?"

The child may answer, "I want a cookie" or "Look how tall I am on the chair." Based on that answer, you can determine which alternative is best. Perhaps the answer is "You can have a cookie after dinner" or "I'll lift you up so that you are taller than me."

If you try to figure it out yourself, both of you may become frustrated because your own biases will seep through. If you automatically assume the child is being rebellious, you will hurt the learning process and possibly impede moving on.

This can be especially dangerous when other people are involved, including siblings and friends. Misinterpreting the child's behavior in front of someone else can be very non-productive. If your child grabs a toy from another child's hand, it may be that the child is being greedy. But the more likely scenario, especially with someone under the age of five, is that that he or she isn't thinking about other people's feelings. The child doesn't have the control to think about how someone else might feel about losing a toy. The solution here is to find a toy that satisfies both children, rather than admonishing them for fighting with each other. The child was not trying to hurt the friend.

As children get older, they may come up with alternatives to the activity they're told not to do. If they are told not to write on the wall, a parent may suggest a coloring book. This may seem like a minor success, however, this positive method of discipline will teach them to color in the book, not to write on the wall again.

Children will experiment and try to push the rules. In fact, that is the kind of behavior you can encourage. Giving children opportunities to think about what they are doing and to explore their options helps them to make good choices. In the long run that is how they will grow. Your children are not perfect and have to learn from their mistakes like the rest of us.

Like Child, Like Flea

Circus trainers are able to control fleas by taking advantage of a flea's negative attitude. Certain kinds of fleas can jump more than 100 times their height, but circus trainers are able to restrict them from jumping so high without even putting a lid on a jar.

Here's how the trainers do it. First, they decide how high they want the fleas to jump. The fleas are placed in a jar with the lid on at just about the same height the trainers want the fleas to jump. For the first few hours, the fleas will jump so high they repeatedly bang their heads against the lid. After a while, the fleas start jumping with less force. Eventually, all of them jump consistently to one inch below the lid to avoid the pain of hitting it.

The flea becomes conditioned to avoid pain and will not jump as high as the lid level. When the trainers take the lid off, the fleas continue to restrict themselves to the same height as if the lid were still on. In fact, the fleas will never jump out – a perfect example of negative conditioning.

If you put a lid on your child's efforts, they are only going to jump so high. Practice Black Belt Parenting and show your children that "the sky's the limit."

Jump!

Chapter 3

But Out!

"And" is a constructive word. "But" is a destructive word. "But" can be replaced with the word "and" in almost any sentence.

Which sentence is negative and which is positive?

1a. I want to let you stay up later, but you're not old enough.

1b. I want to let you stay up later and you will when you're older.

2a. You did the first part of your homework correctly, but the second part is wrong.

2b. You did the first part of your homework correctly and the second part needs a little more work.

"I know you didn't mean to disobey me and I want you to think about that when you are in your room the next three nights."

What comes after the word "and" still isn't necessarily going to be what the other person wants to hear. That happens in most cases, especially when a parent is fulfilling the role of disciplinarian. It's a lot easier for your kids to take what they don't want to hear when the negative is connected to a positive.

"And" serves the same purpose as brakes in a traffic crash.

The crash is bad news and having the brakes prevents a much worse situation. It even affords some relief.

"But" creates a traffic crash. Using the word "but" is like taking someone's argument and running a vehicle into it at a high speed. There is no need for "but" to be there. It doesn't connect two statements. It cuts them in half and places added stress on the second statement, even when the meaning is not intended.

In a debate with your child, inserting the word "but" implies he or she is wrong. It can catapult a minor disagreement into a major argument. Both sides feel their message is being constantly refuted. And in a very real sense, that is correct.

"I'll do my chores later."

"But I told you to do them as soon as you got home from school."

"Yeah, but this is my favorite show."

"I know you love that show, but I expect the dishes to be washed by 6 o'clock."

"They'll be done by 6:30."

"But I planned to start dinner earlier."

It seems that at every turn, someone's "but" is sticking out. The conversation is going nowhere and both sides seem to be getting frustrated. You may even agree partly with what the child is saying. The parent knows the child is watching his or her favorite TV show and the child knows when dinner is supposed to be ready. What's standing in the way of a resolution? You got it—the "but." This going back and forth is enough to make some-one dizzy. A response with a "but" and counter response with another "but" and so on develops into a tornado of words. How can this be resolved? Take out the "but" and insert "and."

Let's rejoin that earlier conversation.

"I'll do my chores later."

"And I told you to do the dishes as soon as you got home from school."

Notice the response is the same. Instead of being a contradic-tion, it is now an extension of what the child previously said about doing those chores. It's easier for the child to agree with the statement because it's not insisting that he or she is wrong. Negotiation and open discussion are now possible. The brakes have been applied and a bad crash is no longer an inevitable event.

Negotiation is necessary to solve the conflict because both sides have competing interests. Working together might result in a solution that makes both sides happy.

The gentle influence of using the word "and" instead of "but" can fit into any conversation. I use it when I talk to parents about how their child is performing in class.

Correct: "Katie is really tough and her willingness to hang in there will help her move up in the long run. She could really use some encouragement."

Incorrect: "Katie is a tough girl, but she is falling behind. She is willing to work hard, but she needs more encouragement."

Three Little Letters—A Big Difference

These two three-letter words can make a big difference in what you say. To play off of Muhammad Ali's famous strategy, "and" floats like a butterfly and "but" stings like a bee. Four-letter words aren't the only ones that rattle the emotions and produce arguments. The correct usage of three-letter words can make the difference between a fight and forgiveness.

Children are very sensitive to the admonishments of a parent. The relationship can be contentious as parents play the role of disciplinarian and it doesn't have to be that way. Children will respond to what you say. Whether they respond in a positive or negative way depends on how you phrase your comments.

Using the word "but" puts a concrete wall between two statements. The meaning of the first statement is lost and the person listening only hears the second part. The words in the second statement might as well be booming out of a microphone decorated with fancy lights and fireworks.

The word "and" serves as a bridge to connect two statements and relate them to one another in a positive way.

"You are a great student and you need to be in class more often." That bridge is easy to cross. The student can use his or her great abilities, as identified in the first part of the sentence, the more often they're in class, as noted in the second part.

"You are a great student, but you need to work on your techniques." With that slight change, the bridge is burned and all the student knows is the flaw. The message that someone is a great student is hidden behind that concrete wall and the need to work on techniques is an ugly flaw staring the student in the face.

"The mind is the limit. As long as the mind can envision the fact that you can do something, you can do it—as long as you really believe 100 percent."

Arnold Schwarzenegger

Attitude Adjustment and Grade Realignment

A classic example of using the word "but" is in examining your child's report card. I don't know about you, but most people are not straight-A students. If most people worked really hard and got B's, they would be quite proud. All of that pride for a job well done could be diminished if someone pointed out that a B is second best. The statement could make someone feel terrible and there are ways to avoid putting someone down who doesn't quite make the mark.

Mrs. Farley's son Pat was normally a great student. He placed well in advanced classes during his freshman year. In the first semester of his sophomore year, though, Pat's English grade dropped from a strong A from the year before to a C+. His other grades remained at the top of the class. Mrs. Farley took a look at her son's report card and said: "You're still doing well, but you got a C in English."

Notice Mrs. Farley set up the sentence with the positive and ended it with a negative. Ultimately, she was expressing disappointment in Pat's grade. The sincerity of the original phrase became lost as soon as the word but popped into the sentence. If her goal was to change Pat's attitude toward his English grade, she succeeded only in throwing a lack of success in his face. She should have adjusted the way she conveyed the need for better grades to a more positive statement.

When the child hears "but", the sincerity of the first phrase is questioned and the child may feel under attack. It is important to toe the line between compliment and criticism so that both messages get through. Your objective is to congratulate your children for a job well done and let them know falling grades in other subjects is not acceptable.

Tell them in this format: "You did a great job and this English grade could use improvement."

Think how Mrs. Farley's statements could affect Pat's thoughts. He might think "I'm bad at English. I can't do it. I'm not good enough." Don't let those thoughts resonate in your child's head. Redirect their mental circuits to his or her strengths. Soon, your child will stop mulling over failures. Instead he or she will be championing abilities and applying them to the areas that need improvement.

For example, "If I work as hard in English as I did in algebra, I will get a better grade." That seems easy enough. However, other emotions could be at work if, for example, Pat did work hard in English and still didn't do as well as expected. In that case, he needs to be motivated to take that next step and work harder.

Make sure your children understand that the task at hand can be done and you are willing to stick by them through the process.

Mrs. Farley could say, "I found English a challenge in high school, too. I got a tutor who really helped me and I'd like to get you a tutor. Would you agree to that?"

Since getting tutored isn't always fun, it may be worthwhile to add some sort of reward to tutoring. For example, after each session the child can stay up an hour later that night or get cookies during tutoring. I was never did well in English class. If I had associated it with cookies, though, I'm willing to bet a chocolate chip cookie that I'd have my old English book practically memorized. Tutoring day would turn into cookie day and that's something to look forward to. If children have a positive attitude toward doing work, they are more likely to comprehend it.

Breaking Old Habits

The old saying "Sticks and stones may break my bones, but words will never hurt me" is not correct. Sticks and stones can break bones. However, most conflicts never get so far as to cause physical harm. But words flung in a conflict may make a mental impact. They can hurt.

Your objective is to help your child. Do not concentrate on flaws or accentuate them. This will only lead them to re-create the same behavior. It would be foolish if in an effort to improve your child's behavior, he ended up concentrating on his flaws and putting himself down.

Basketball great Michael Jordan said, "You have to expect things of yourself before you can do them." You have to expect things of your children before they can expect things of themselves. Once that ball is in the air, it become a three-point long shot from mid-court headed right into the basket.

You are what you think you are. If the child is taught to concentrate on the negative, he or she makes that negative a self-fulfilling prophecy.

I had a student, Ray, who was fast, intelligent and talented. He had a real natural talent and placed high at tournaments. In class, though, his dedication faded. He did not practice his techniques and frequently messed them up in tests. It was especially frustrating to see him mess up an easy technique because I knew that students with a lower rank looked up to him.

Ray would brush it off and he did not make any efforts to get it right after he was corrected. This went on for months. I kept telling him, "You have a lot of talent, but you have to practice your techniques."

Ray continued to hone his natural talent and snapped super fast kicks in complicated competition katas. He was able to perform some of the really advanced moves, too. However, his attention to detail in understanding the art of karate continued to be lacking. And his effort to nail down defense techniques was non-existent. He would basically "go through the motions" so it appeared he was trying until we reached the part of class in which he excelled.

After he failed a promotion test because he didn't know his techniques, I asked him why he didn't practice them. His response was, "I'm not good at techniques. I don't like them."

I was at a loss for words. I knew that if he would practice them as much as he did his kicks, he would be great. It became my mission to show him that. At a seminar in Las Vegas two weeks later, I told the speaker my concern about Ray.

"Ray is a smart, talented boy. He is always pushing his limits with the kicks and katas, but he never listens or puts forth effort when we go over self defense techniques," I said.

Immediately, the motivational speaker said, "Aha! I can tell why he is not motivated. It's because you're not telling him how to get better."

I was absolutely insulted. I always try to be a positive influence. I started to defend myself, "But, I..."

He cut me off and said, "That's it. You said 'but.'" Don't use that word when you talk about him or to him. Telling him he's great, BUT he needs to work on techniques is separating techniques from greatness. 'But' is standing in the way."

Even though I had been telling Ray he was talented at kicks, Ray did not make the connection that he could also be great at techniques using that same talent. Why? I had built a wall called "but" in between the two sentences. Ray heard me when I said he was great at kicks. He knew that. However, I wasn't properly sending the message that techniques could be mastered as an extension of his talent.

I returned from Las Vegas early Monday morning with the intention of sleeping off the plane ride and leaving class up to other instructors. I was so eager to try out what I had learned in Las Vegas, though, I could hardly sleep. I decided to go to class because I knew Ray would be in, as he usually came to class on Mondays and Wednesdays. I didn't want to wait till the middle of the week to start making a difference.

As soon as we broke up into groups to go over techniques, I made a special effort to tell Ray, "You are a great martial artist and I'm glad you are practicing that technique." Instead of sticking "but" in the middle of the statement I used "and".

I built a bridge in Ray's mind instead of a wall. How did that change Ray's thinking? It connected the two thoughts that a martial artist and tournament champion practices techniques. He practiced a little more that day and over the next two weeks I did not let up. I made special efforts to point out his ability at techniques. Wouldn't you know, he started practicing them with the same fervor with which he practiced kicks and competition katas.

Promotion Emotion

The prospect of promotion is a great motivator for my students. They look forward to moving up in rank and promotion nights are always special events for those participating. The parents crowd the visitor's area with cameras and proudly watch their children demonstrate the moves needed to step up in rank. At the end of the ceremony, students take off their old belts and strap on the new ones to resounding applause. Many times parents, friends and relatives who don't usually bring the child to class show up for these events. For many people, it marks the first time they've seen the child practice karate.

Before the ceremony, we test the children to make sure they are prepared to perform their techniques and to qualify for the next rank. It is not an effort to point out what they don't know, but an opportunity for them to show off what they do know. This is a great time because the students are happy to have visitors and the visitors are impressed with the students' abilities. The room is usually crowded with gushing parents and beaming, energetic children.

I use promotion nights as an opportunity to teach friends and relatives methods to motivate children at home. I want to improve the lives of everyone who steps into my school even once and to provide some nugget of knowledge they can apply to improve their own lives. Promotion nights are a great opportunity for me to reach out to more people.

I carefully select my lessons on promotion nights so they apply to both students and parents. Since I have the attention of a larger audience than usual, I struggle to make sure this lesson will be meaningful. I try to draw examples from real life and one night I was able to do that after hearing an altercation between a student, Chris, and his father, Mr. Jacobus.

Chris advanced from his orange belt to purple belt at the ceremony. The rank of purple belt also pushed him from the beginner class into the black belt training course, so it was a special milestone. Mr. Jacobus had been on the sidelines throughout Chris' training and usually watched him practice in class. He was disappointed that Chris wasn't very sharp on one of the techniques. As soon as the ceremony ended, Chris ran off the training floor to his dad. The conversation went something like this:

"Why did you hesitate on that last technique, 'Striking Asp'?" Mr. Jacobus asked.

"I don't know. I forgot it," said Chris.

"But you had plenty of time to practice."

"I know it. I just messed up."

"I know you had it right before, but you're a purple belt now and shouldn't be messing up."

Mr. Jacobus used the word "but" several times and the excitement of getting the belt had dissipated for Chris. He didn't feel like he accomplished anything because his dad told him that, in essence, he wasn't a true purple belt.

It was clear to me that Chris knew the technique because he had done it flawlessly in class several times to qualify for his purple belt. He probably made a mistake because he was in front of an audience and had developed a mild form of stage fright. It was a slight mistake and his father was probably the only person who noticed.

Mr. Jacobus approached me and said that his son was practicing at home, but he did not have the moves down. I knew he did not mean to negate his son's accomplishments. I told him that it was okay for students to make mistakes as long as they worked to improve them. Even though Chris was behind in doing "Striking Asp," he finished the technique and executed the rest of his techniques in class.

I told Mr. Jacobus to encourage Chris to practice the orange belt techniques in front of him at home to get him accustomed to performing before an audience. I also told him that concentrating on that mistake was, as the saying goes, missing the forest for the trees. Mr. Jacobus had every reason to be proud of his son and I encouraged him not to lose sight of that. Chris worked very hard to earn his purple belt and he needed to know he deserved it without any "buts."

Mr. Jacobus later told his son, "Chris, now that you're a purple belt, children in the beginner class will look up to you. Let's practice to make sure you know all your moves perfectly!" Mr. Jacobus did just that and he wasn't disappointed in Chris again. Even if Chris made a mistake, his father learned to cushion the blow with the word "and" instead of "but." When Chris made a mistake in class a few weeks later, I heard Mr. Jacobus say, "You have the first part of the kata correct and you'll nail down the second part after a few more days of practice."

That's exactly what Chris needed to hear. And that's Black Belt Parenting.

The word "but" often precedes negative news. If you heard "I know you want a raise, but ..." What would you expect to hear after that? The rejection of the raise would probably come next.

"I know you want a raise, but we can't afford to give everyone more money. Sales are down."

That's a big set-up for a big let-down. There are better ways of getting across bad news. Putting a bright slant on it may soften the blow.

"I know you want a raise and I really appreciate your hard work, so the next time I can free up money from the powers that be, I will write you a check. Business is a little slower this year and I know you deserve more money. It may take a little more time. We do owe much of our success to your hard work and if you could wait just a little longer, I think that can be arranged."

That's not the same as cash in your pocket, true. However, the unfortunate message put in a more positive light will prevent aggravation and resentment. Using "but" would have made for a real adversarial relationship.

One summer, I was in the ticket line at the airport on my way to a seminar in Florida. Airports can be very stressful and I saw tempers hit a boiling point between a customer service representative and a customer. The man had bought a ticket for a flight scheduled to leave 45 minutes later, but was already delayed by 30 minutes. The irate customer complained that he had to get on an earlier plane to make a business meeting.

The airline representative replied, "I see, but we don't have any flights leaving earlier. All flights to Florida are delayed due to thunderstorms."

"How could this happen? The weather is fine in Florida," the man replied.

"Yes, but flights got backed up earlier and there won't be air space until later," the agent said.

"But my meeting starts in a few hours. What kind of airline is this?" the man said.

"But we have to get other passengers waiting since this morning on a plane."

The fight went on and on. The airline couldn't do anything about the delay and the man was going to be late, but the small war of words continued.

The customer wouldn't accept the situation because he was only hearing the excuses, not the explanation. Eventually, the airline representative called another employee to deal with other customers in line and I got through without a hitch. As I lugged my bags to the terminal, I thought about how roadblocks stood at every corner of that conversation. Both the airline representative and the customer resorted to "buts" that kept the conflict from reaching a satisfactory resolution. They could have gotten the plane off the ground by pushing it down the runway easier than they could have solved their conflict through those three-letter words.

Think about this airport scenario the next time you are being dragged into a no-win confrontation with someone. We can practice Black Belt Parenting. We can really communicate with our children. We can teach and we can learn.

If only we can get our heads out of our "buts!"

Chapter 4

Preparation

"I will prepare and some day my chance will come."
Abraham Lincoln
16th President of the United States

Pre-framing

Pre- *(prefix) 1. Earlier than: prior to before 2. Preparatory or pre-requisite.*
Webster's Ninth New Collegiate Dictionary

Framing (v) 1. To construct; build. 2. To design; draw up. 3. To arrange or adjust for a purpose ...
American Heritage Dictionary

Framing (v) 1. To form according to a pattern; design. 2. To construct 3. To put into words.
Webster's New World Dictionary

Framing (v) – Benefit ... make progress.
Webster's Ninth New Collegiate Dictionary

Pre-Framing

Framing is a verb. That means it's an action word and it requires effort. Pre-framing is character building by drawing an image in someone's head that benefits that individual as he or she makes progress prior to actually making the progress. It is developing a pattern for success as a prerequisite to achieving it. Pre-framing describes or anticipates a positive future based on what someone is doing now.

Pre-framing is an important concept I use on a daily basis to motivate people. In all of our karate classes, pre-framing prepares students for the next step in their journey to black belt status.

Everything we do at each class level lays the framework for the next step. In the beginner class, basic kicks get them started. Those basic kicks become spin kicks in the black belt training course. And those spin kicks become jump-spin kicks in the advanced class. The next goal is black belt and the goal beyond that is black belt excellence. How excellent can you get? The sky is the limit. It is a never-ending cycle of improvement.

In martial arts, excellence is all about taking knowledge from one part of training and applying it to the next. You don't train for hours each week and then wake up one day as a black belt. Katas (series of moves strung together to make a routine) improve self defense techniques, which improve sparring, which improve katas, and so on. The experience accumulates and each step of the journey is one of many challenges that gets you there. You don't graduate high school and miraculously become a college student. You first learn basics in elementary school and build on those throughout primary education. You evolve to the next level rather than taking a flying leap. We use pre-framing in every single class on every level – not just in the context of earning a black belt. For example, I tell the students, "If you master this kick, you'll be awesome in tomorrow's class."

Pre-framing is multi-layered with each goal overlapping over time.

"You don't run 26 miles at five minutes a mile on good looks and a secret recipe," said Frank Shorter, after he won the Gold medal at the 1972 Olympics marathon.
Shorter's words are true for all sports. I'd also add that you don't raise good kids with good looks and a secret recipe. You can't wait for time to pass and expect success to fall in your lap. You've got to earn tomorrow's success today.

"The best preparation for good work tomorrow is to do good work today."

Elbert Hubbard

Pre-school Pre-framing

Pre-framing begins early. My partner, Miss Jacque, teaches the three and four year old Asah Sharks with the same philosophy. The class of energetic tots is ecstatic to wear a gi, or karate uniform, and class is playtime for them. It is a great opportunity to introduce pre-framing so that it comes naturally as they get older and prepare for the next stages in their training. If they learn early to expect their work to pay off with future benefits, that frame of mind will stick with them throughout life.

Miss Jacque tells the Sharks to put on imaginary black belts so they kick like black belts—not like untrained kids. It is remarkable how the children respond to this technique. They smile brightly and imagine they are kicking as black belt champions. Pretending they are wearing black belts makes them feel stronger and in fact they actually act stronger. They even talk to each other jokingly about their new belt.

"Check out my black belt!" the children say to each other, pointing to belts of all different colors. They have fun imagining the future achievement of the real thing. This is the first step in teaching children at such a young age that a black belt means excellence. Starting early puts them on the right track to respond to pre-framing in the future.

As beginners they are not ready to go through extensive testing and perform complex moves. They are, however, being pre-framed to expect a higher level of performance at each step until a black belt is reached. We teach that you can perform like a black belt at every level. We have several students who started at age three or four who went on to earn their adult black belts. They continue training to this day. They don't know what pre-framing is or how it affects them and at the same time their attitude toward improving is positive as a direct result of pre-framing. I like to say that all of our students are black belts from the moment they hit the training floor—they just haven't earned the belt yet.

"Spectacular achievement is always preceded by spectacular preparation."

Robert H. Schuller

Pre-framing is a great technique to motivate children to stick with whatever activity they pursue. Whether it's something as important as the lifestyle of martial arts, playing the piano, soccer, or chess, pre-framing establishes the benefits of an activity and encourages the child to continue through to reach the upper levels of the benefits.

Think about the Asah Sharks who learn early that it's best to kick like a black belt. That develops confidence, strength and self-discipline. The black belt represents the epitome of these great characteristics and stopping short of that goal is giving up too soon. When parents tell me their child is considering dropping out, I tell them that it is important to make sure the child follows through on any goals he or she has set.

When parents enroll for a certain karate program, it is important that the child follows through and completes the goal, whether it is a blue belt or black belt. Reminding the child of the goal at every stage of the game is pre-framing and helps keep him or her motivated.

It's natural for people to think toward the future as a better time. Using that same mind set, motivate your children to do the right things now so that their vision of the future becomes reality. Working hard in school and having a positive attitude about the work prepares them for a lifetime of success. The more preparation, the smoother the sailing when future challenges show up.

Allowing children to bail out early sends the message that it's okay to give up on a goal. It may set a precedent so that they think they can give up on anything. This behavior won't serve them well later in life when they pursue a romantic relationship, educational advancement or a career.

Consider the age-old complaint of high school students: I will never need to use algebra later in my life so why do I need to learn it now? This is an opportunity to teach them the value of using their minds critically in complex math and formulaic situations, which they in fact will encounter in the future. It may be a losing cause to sing the praises of algebra as applicable in of itself to a future career. As a karate instructor, I'm confident I haven't used algebra since high school. However, using that part of my brain to solve algebra equations prepared me for the complicated world of running a business.

Tell the child, "If you do your homework, you will be ready for next year's challenges. You will have practiced using critical thinking in other classes which gives you knowledge to land a great job."

There's always a reason for doing your best at everything.

The Grass Is Always Greener...

If you are a typical optimist, the future always looks brighter. It starts at a young age and continues each year. What is accomplished is soon forgotten as we begin thinking about the achievements ahead. The preschooler can't wait to go to the "big kids" school. Grade school children want to play sports like the middle school children. Those in middle school look up to the high-school students who drive and date. The high-school kids anticipate freedom and independence in college and college students look forward to financial independence and a good job.

It doesn't end there. Adults see better financial security as they move up the corporate ladder. Financial independence is always one promotion away. When the children grow up and move away, life will be easier. Then retirement becomes the next, best thing. Soon you are long-retired and looking to the future turns into looking at the glory days of the past. Ironically, in the past you weren't concentrating on how good things were at the moment. You were contemplating a distant future—where you are now.

However, this can trap people into forgetting about all of the great things in the present. As each stage of life slowly morphs into the next, don't forget to recognize the goals and milestones reached. As you raise your children, appreciate the success you've had in getting through school and starting a family and how pre-framing prepared you for the excellent parent you are today. Being a Black Belt Parent doesn't start when the child is born. It starts with learning how to take responsibility in your earlier years and being a good example. Each stage in life is not a clean slate.

If you're able to visualize how your behavior will affect and improve your life, you will better prepared to make the right decision. Hey, if it worked for Ebeneezer Scrooge, it can work for you. In Charles Dickens' novel <u>A Christmas Carol</u> Scrooge is given a unique look at his life. The ghost of Christmas Past showed scrooge how his past behavior turned him into a stingy old man. The ghost of Christmas Present showed him current events he had managed to overlook. The ghost of Christmas Future showed him possible outcomes if he didn't change his behavior. Once he saw his options, the grumpy character decided to change his ways and vowed to be kinder.

Since we don't have the luxury of a storybook's perspective on our own lives, take the advice of someone who did, Ebeneezer Scrooge. Recognize the lessons in everyday life and pass them on to your children so they will have a strong foundation to become whatever they strive to be. Take a lesson from Scrooge who said, "I will live in the Past, the Present, and the Future. The Spirits of all Three shall strive within me. I will not shut out the lessons that they teach."

Take some time to think about how your behavior now might help or hurt your chances of reaching the next milestone in your life. Will watching sitcoms for two hours a day help you get a promotion? Will allowing your children to watch three hours of cartoons a day in elementary school prepare them for hours of homework in middle school or high school?

Since people naturally think the future is going to be better, use that belief to motivate your child to do the right things now. It doesn't matter what you want to be. What matters is the kind of person you're going to be and how well you do what you set out to do. If you want to be successful you have start now and never give up.

"Education is our passport to the future, for tomorrow belongs to the people who prepare for it today."

Malcolm X

Pre-Punching

In karate, an example of pre-framing is having the students jump high in an intermediate class. This prepares their muscles for later jumps and kicks. To some, jumping may seem juvenile or unrelated to karate.

One mother angrily said, "Why is Noel jumping up and down in place? That's not karate!"

I told her that practicing high jumps now prepares them for the next step in their training. In all classes, students know that earning their black belt is the ultimate goal and everything they do every time they train brings them one step closer to reaching that goal.

That's Black Belt Excellence.

I work hard to keep the black belt in the forefront of their minds at all times. That is pre-framing. It is important to keep all of your child's goals at the forefront of his or her mind and to associate every action with having an effect on that goal. If one goal is getting straight A's, every homework assignment is preparation to earn a better grade.

"Hey, I see you're doing your geometry homework. Great job!

That hard work will definitely be reflected in your report card."

One of our goals when we spar is to improve all of our karate skills and to use those skills in the ring. One way we do this is by practicing drills wearing full gear: mouthpiece, head gear, feet gear, hand gear and shin pads. They practice everything including punch combinations, moving around the ring and blocking hits. Students may not get into hand-to-hand combat in their sparring gear. They are paired off in twos, and do something as simple as knee lifts or squats—moves that certainly would not earn them a point in a sparring match.

One father asked me why the class was wasting its time doing something that couldn't turn over directly into sparring points.

I told him, "Obviously when they're sparring, squats won't do them much except tire them out. They're not at the advanced stage where they are able to move effortlessly around the ring and land points. Getting them used to all different positions that resemble parts of kicks or ducks while in gear with their hands up is the first step. This way, they won't all of a sudden have to add a whole new element to their sparring when they reach the higher level and have to scramble with all kind of moves around the ring. If they practice now, they will already feel comfortable getting into awkward positions they're not used to and won't hesitate to do it when the time is right."

Without using the word, I told him we were pre-framing for black belt success.

Smoke and Mirrors

Every negative thing you do now is like smoking - it will eventually catch up with you. Smoking is an easy example because the hazards are so clear and also dependent on time.

I caught one of our 16-year-old students behind the school smoking a cigarette before class. At the time, Ed was a brown belt in the advanced class who liked to rebel and would occasionally make a smart-aleck comment. When he saw me coming, he put out the cigarette. I asked why he was smoking.

"It's no big deal," Ed said.

I reminded him that smoking was dangerous to his health.

"It doesn't matter. I can still do everything in class. I'm doing just as good at school and karate as I was before I started smoking," he said.

"You're right," I said. The truth is that I'm sure the bright kid did well in school and he was progressing very nicely at karate. He was right that smoking wasn't hurting his abilities at the moment, but he wasn't thinking about how smoking was affecting him on the inside.

"Do you want to earn your black belt in a few years?" I asked.

"Yeah, and I will. It's not like I'm 'gonna quit karate because I smoke."

"Smoking slows you down and cuts off your ability to breathe. You won't be able to train as hard and the workouts aren't going to get any easier. Smoking will catch up with you. Have you ever seen a smoker go up the stairs and become winded? You have to be better than that to pass the black belt test," I said.

"But smoking gives me energy in the morning and I don't eat as much so I'm in better shape," he said.

I explained that those side effects were temporary and that smoking eventually slows people down. I asked him if these current so-called benefits were worth giving up on his future goals.

"No, but I said I'm not going to give up," Ed said.

"Picture yourself as a black belt. Now picture yourself as a black belt with a cigarette in your mouth. Does that look right to you?" I asked.

"I guess not. I'm only smoking a little bit anyway," he said.

Ed had to learn the lesson that current behavior affects future performance. He didn't think of any of the dangers of smoking because none were apparent at the moment. He didn't see the tar sticking to his lungs, his clothes were still fresh and his breath was passable.

"Why are you training so hard now?" I asked.

"So I can get better and be a black belt," Ed said, right on point.

"Obviously, then, you see how what you do now affects how you're able to do things later," I said. "It's the same thing with smoking."

Ed was speechless. He was known for his comebacks and this

time he didn't have one. He suddenly realized that every time he smoked, he brought himself one step closer to an unhealthy life. Ed had already been exposed to the concept of pre-framing in how his parents raised him and how we taught him at karate. He probably gave in to peer group pressure when he started smoking. He needed a reminder of why smoking is such a bad idea. Thankfully, he realized that there are more important things to life than puffing on cancer sticks and he went on to earn his black belt.

If you smoke now and end up on an oxygen tank in 25 years, then you'll know how your behavior pre-framed your future. If you stay in good shape, 25 years from now you'll be active and feel younger than your years.

While keeping an eye on the future rewards of today's work, remember that today's work is also its own reward.

A great way to put pre-framing into perspective is to think of segments in broadcast news programs called "teasers." Right before a commercial break, news programs "tease" an upcoming story without giving away the heart of the story. It keeps the viewers interested and sets them up for what is coming.

Teasers are especially important in the news because each broadcast is so different. People don't know what to expect. In other television programs, people have a reasonable idea of what kind of drama will unfold on the other side of a commercial break. If you're interested in the story plot of a soap opera, sitcom or sports game, there's a reasonably high chance you will stick around for the rest of the show. When it comes to the news, the segment before the commercial break may be about a double murder, but the show returns to a segment on the local fair, sports scores, weather forecast or medical breakthrough.

Pre-framing gives the viewer an opportunity to get a sneak peak at what is coming up so they hopefully decide that what's ahead will be interesting. After watching the first half of a news program one night, I was ready to flip off the television when the news anchor teased a story on fitness.

"Coming up, is your fitness routine the right fit? Stay tuned to find out some of the hottest trends in fitness that may work for you." As the female anchor talked, images of buff people in tight clothes using odd workout devices flashed on the screen. There was no treadmill, aerobics class or weight bench. Working out has always been a part of my life and although I was sleepy I stayed tuned and waited another 15 minutes before the segment came on. It was worth the wait. A dietician talked about cardio kick-boxing, a program we've done at our school for years. It was enlightening to see a new perspective on the subject. Without that tease I wouldn't have watched the segment.

When I teach katas, students don't learn the series of 15 to 50 moves in one day. They comprehend best using the pyramid style of teaching. After each new move, you return to the beginning and practice up to the new point. As time goes on and each move is added, the students are able to build on it and remember the kata. Their minds are pre-framed to learn this way and I depend on repeating what works. It is the best and fastest way to learn and have the information stick.

On The Other Side

Pre-framing is about showing the child that hard work can give you a nice house, respect, a successful career and much more. Pre-framing is not only about showing your children the positive rewards of hard work. It's also about showing them the dismal alternative if they don't work hard. Take them to a really nice neighborhood or a car dealership and show them what their future hard work can buy. While pushing a materialistic agenda is not a good idea, children respond well to concepts applied visually.

A good friend of mine, Harold, worked his way up from living in a very undesirable neighborhood to a nice home on the main line in Philadelphia. He did his best to make sure his children enjoyed the finer things in life. They lived in a nice house, rode in top-of-the-line cars and ate at nice restaurants. His children, Marc and Alison, go to a private school. However, Harold made sure they knew his roots so they would not take their situation for granted.

For his son's 11th birthday, Harold bought Marc a new bike. The next day, Harold found the $300 present on the ground in the driveway. Luckily, it didn't rain. But Harold was angry that Marc didn't appreciate the value of the gift and take care of it. He discovered there were scrapes on the handle bars and that Marc had not even attempted to use the kickstand.

When Marc heard that hard work would earn him a better life, he had no way of visualizing that beyond what he wanted the next day. To teach his son a lesson, Harold drove Marc about 20 minutes away to the poorest section of town. Marc never been there and typically Harold wouldn't want his son going there. However, a strong dose of harsh reality was just what the doctor ordered.

During the hour-long drive, Harold explained what he went through growing up and said that Marc's future was not set in stone. Harold talked about the conditions in the ghetto, how easy it is to get there and how hard it is to get out. He said the trip was necessary because Marc did not seem to appreciate how good he had it. The vision of what life is like on the other side motivated Marc to begin earning that good life. Trips through degenerated neighborhoods were necessary a few more times over the next couple years to keep Marc's head straight. Each trip hammered home the point. Harold's ability to keep Marc's head out of the clouds and feet on the ground is the work of a great dad—a real Black Belt Parent.

I think it is appropriate to end this chapter on pre-framing with a quote from Lord Baden Powell: "Be prepared."

Chapter 5

Must It Up

At several seminars, I've heard the speakers say, "Don't should all over yourself." It is pointless to mention what someone should've done because it is impossible to control the past. So don't say "'Ya, 'shoulda..." and expect your children to work any time-traveling miracles! Leave "should" where it belongs—in the past. Black Belt Parents live in the present and look into the future.

Using the word should forces children to relive the negative incident by reminding them of their mistake. Just as you cannot go back and do things you should've done, your child is bound by the rules of time and place. That may seem like an unnecessary statement, but consider how many times you've thought, "I should've bought batteries while I was at the store," or "I should've spent more time with him while I had the chance." These are natural thoughts. However, it is unfair to bind yourself to the past and it is unnecessary to do that to your children. It sets an unrealistic precedent.

Consider this situation. Hugh McNabb was having a bad day. His alarm didn't go off and he got a late start. He missed his first-period class. At lunchtime, he realized he forgot his geometry assignment, so he tried to rush back home to pick it up. As soon as he drove onto the street, he was stuck behind a school bus. By the time he dashed home and then returned to school, he missed his geometry class. He tried to explain this to his teacher, Mrs. Mervine when he got back. She was not interested in any excuses.

"You should have brought your homework to school with you this morning," she said.

Now, what are Hugh's options? He already knows he should have remembered his geometry assignment, but, unfortunately, he didn't. His options appear limited.

Mrs. Mervine's comment sets up an impossible task. When you think about it, Hugh doesn't have any options. He certainly can't go back in time. And Mrs. Mervine isn't giving him the option to fix the future. The teacher failed to teach Hugh a valuable lesson when she had the chance. This is frustrating because she won't be appeased and Hugh can't correct his mistake.

Here are some alternative responses that would have helped the situation.

"You woke up late today? Tomorrow, you must wake up an hour early to come into the computer lab and do an extra assignment to make up for the class you missed."

"I suggest you buy a back-up alarm clock that runs on batteries and you must not be late to another class this semester."

"Since your assignment is late, I will not accept it. You must come to class early every day next week to work on a make-up assignment."

"It is class policy that if you are not present, I will not accept an assignment. I have to give you a grade of zero. You must be here on time in every class for the next month and I will erase it from your record."

Notice in all of these options, Hugh can actually do something and take an action. He's still not off the hook, though. This is the kind of balance teachers strive to reach – teaching a student a lesson at the same time punishment is given. That same balance needs to be worked out in the home.

Instead of "This is what you should've done," say "This is what you could do in the future." Provide the child with an option to act positively.

At a recent test for his brown belt, Roy showed up unprepared. His gi was wrinkled and he forgot his belt. When his mom asked why he looked like that, Roy said, "My teacher gave us an extra assignment two days ago and I didn't have time to iron my gi."

"You should've done it earlier instead of waiting until the last minute."

"I know I should've done it, but I thought I'd have time," Roy said. His mom was disappointed because she usually takes a lot of pictures of him at tests and she thinks Roy will look disheveled. He wishes he had ironed his gi, but he can't go back and change that.

"You must change uniforms. Find something else to wear. You can't test in that," she said.

It may not be what he wanted to hear, but Roy was given an option. That's something he can do in the here-and-now. He can't go back and iron his uniform, but he can try to find something else to wear to address his mother's disappointment.

Roy decided he would borrow a gi from someone in the class. Even though Roy was embarrassed, his mom insisted that he ask his friends who weren't testing if he could borrow a clean uniform. No one had the right size gi. As Roy was running out of options, he finally told me about his dilemma. I knew he was ready to test and I didn't want his mom to be upset. I also didn't want to let Roy off the hook.

So I gave Roy a brand new crisp uniform on one condition: He had to earn it. For the next four weeks, Roy was to come in an hour early to help clean the school. Coming in early every week would be a learning experience for him. At the same time, he knew he was there because he had to look presentable at special events. Roy actually started ironing his gi twice a week because he didn't want to get stuck in that same situation again.

When you are disappointed that your child did something he or she shouldn't have done, tie the punishment into future accomplishment. In this case, Roy's punishment reminded him to keep up with his appearance as well as fostering a sense of responsibility.

Must In Games

I first started using the word must instead of should on a regular basis when we played games in class, such as relay races and mini-sports competitions. For the longest time, I considered games optional. Sure, I encouraged the students to be supportive of each other, but I didn't require them to cheer on their teammates or help them out.

In games where the champion is determined by a team effort, I would tell the class, "You should high-five your teammates." Not everyone followed directions. At times, there would be a few energetic children eager to congratulate each other, but there were no standard high-fives, congratulations, or encouraging thumbs up.

I was under the impression that if they didn't want to cheer for the team, they didn't have to because "it's just a game" and not part of their karate curriculum. Besides, they all seemed to have fun individually. Since they looked forward to playing games I didn't want to spoil the fun by forcing rules on them.

One day during a relay race, I noticed that both teams were sitting there doing nothing while one person rushed down the training area and ran back. I thought, "What a waste! This is valuable class time and they need to be more supportive." I remembered that I had always found half the fun of playing team sports is being on a team. I started to slowly inject requirements into games by changing my vocabulary.

"You must high-five all of your teammates after your turn."

Amazingly, the strategy didn't take away any of the entertainment aspect of the drills. In fact, it added a whole new dimension of playing! It may seem strange that it would take effort to encourage children to enjoy a game more. What stopped them from that next level of team spirit is that the group was too shy to share their excitement with each other. They weren't used to that sort of communication in school or other activities. They were used to focusing on individual abilities and performance. The overall accomplishments of the team became lost in self-interest. I laugh when I think about the times my younger brother would sulk when his team scored a point – because he didn't land the goal himself.

In class games students would think, "Why do I have to high-five my teammates? We're not even winning. Who cares?"

Soon, they were no longer given the opportunity to ask those questions. High-fives became part of the game. Anyone who didn't join in enthusiastically wouldn't be part of the first place team.

After this system was in place for a few weeks, I noticed that some students got so wound up giving high-fives and hanging out with teammates that they weren't following along and were even missing their turn. Going from one end of the spectrum to the other was an unintended consequence of my plan. They were so caught up in the teamwork that they forgot themselves as individuals! I wasn't discouraged. After seeing how well changing my vocabulary worked to encourage teamwork, I resolved that I could use the same strategy to give students a sense of individual accomplishment *within the team.*

The next time we held relay races, each of the two teams lined up and waited while the person in front of them ran down the training area, did marching front kicks, ten push-ups, ten jumping jacks and then ran back to the line and high fived their teammates. This is where the breakdown in the game occurred. Once a student high fives the team and sits down there was no more direction. He or she would talk in line, play or wrestle other members, or be otherwise distracted. I'd tell them, "You should sit together in a straight line like a team." Occasionally they showed self-discipline and lined up. Other times, they took the advice like a suggestion they could choose to accept or ignore. That's when I added more musts to my instructions.

"You must sit with your legs crossed while you are waiting for your team to finish." They understood that. It is a simple explanation of what they are supposed to do so they weren't left to haphazardly do their own thing. Now if they don't high-five teammates then sit together, they can't win the race. Sitting essentially became a competition and they hardly realized that they were sitting nicely instead of jumping around.

Must Be A Black Belt

The weeks leading up to the black belt test are the apex of

training. That's when everyone is expected to be sharp. Excellent physical conditioning and mental preparation is required to hold one of the most recognized ranks in the world. In addition, black belt candidates are expected to write an essay, read a book, show up to class on time and exhibit self-discipline.

Students who reach the black belt level have completed countless hours of training. Sometimes I become so accustomed to their individual talents, rebellions and personalities, I don't enforce uniform guidelines for the black belt test. In past tests, I told the class they should do all of those extra requirements with reading and writing. By using the word should, I left room for students who are comfortable around me to skirt the rules. Some students took advantage of that situation and created a split between those who did the work and those who chose not to. I didn't think it was fair that some students did all of that extra work while others moved along and earned the same reward.

Also, those who weren't doing the work weren't learning the valuable lessons in the assigned books. And they weren't learning more about themselves and articulating what is important about the black belt in their own words. I decided this was too important a milestone to let it slide. I started saying, "You must read a book and write an essay." That meant it was part of being a black belt.

Students who probably would have ignored the suggestions had I said "should" do the assignment were stressing out about the essay. One student, Edgar, brought in a new version every week for two months prior to the deadline because he was so nervous about getting it right. Another student, Alana, was so caught up in figuring out what book to read that she used up her allowance buying three books to make sure one would be good enough. If they were dedicated enough to go through all of the training to earn their black belt, they weren't going to let these other requirements stand in their way. But, in some cases, they weren't necessarily going to volunteer to do the extra work.

I kept using the new vocabulary when I talked to students about other rules they were bending. "You must show up on time." "You must practice this kata tonight so you're ready for the test tomorrow." If the word should is used, children feel as if they have the option to disregard the advice. Saying that things "must" be done improved the rate of compliance dramatically. Imagine if your children, boss or spouse followed all of the rules and complied with your wishes. I'm proud to say my students have met the challenge.

Parents need to use must not only when talking to kids, but when talking to themselves. When you walk past a Baskin Robbins and are trying to keep on your diet, don't say, "I shouldn't eat this." Sure, you shouldn't, but you want to and you immediately start making up excuses.

"I shouldn't eat this, but I didn't eat dessert for the last two days."

"I shouldn't eat this, but I haven't had Baskin Robbins ice cream in months."

"I shouldn't eat this, but I'm really craving it right at this moment."

If you allow your mind to go through those ideas, you'll soon be saying, "I shouldn't have eaten that."

The phrase to remember is *I must not,* as in "I must not stop at the Baskin Robbins." There is no room for judgment. The only option is to walk (or run) past the ice cream parlor. Using the word should in the past tense makes people feel frustrated. If someone told you that you should've done something, do you feel relieved? Can you do anything about it? Well, don't frustrate other people by using that same language.

I have to admit that there are times when I have used 'should' about things I meant to do – even after I eliminated the word from my class vocabulary. When I thought about things I should do, I ended up leaving those responsibilities hanging. Using should gave me a crutch instead of no excuse for getting done what I wanted to get done. In fact, the book you hold in your hands is the final product of my determination to turn a should into a must.

I wanted to write this book for a long time, but I kept procrastinating. I second-guessed my ability to write. I somehow convinced myself I was busier than I actually was. Still, I had the nagging feeling that writing this book could have a great impact on many parents. I buckled down, stopped using "shoulds" to block my success, and finally wrote <u>Black Belt Parenting</u>. I didn't want to go to sleep one more night not doing what I must do.

Don't let your time constraints change you. Don't let them dominate you. Make the time. Anything that you think you should do, you can do—if you put your mind to it. Set every goal with a must.

Many people use "should" when they make excuses not to exercise.

"I know I should get in better shape, but I work a lot of overtime." That's just an excuse. If you found the time to work overtime, you can find the time to exercise. Everyone knows they should exercise, but they don't get up the motivation to do it. When you are out of practice, sweating it out on a bike does not seem like a lot of fun. However, if you worked out for all those times you shoved the idea into the "should" pile, the excuses would no longer be there. It would be part of your daily life and something you looked forward to and something to be proud of.

How many times have you thought, "I should get in shape?" It's a common goal and almost as common are the failures to reach it. Change that attitude to "I must get in shape" and you'll be on your way. Attach it to something that means a lot to you,

"I must get in shape to look great at my child's wedding." If getting in shape is important to you, the motivation of imagining yourself in a form-fitting gorgeous dress or your old tux at a special event will do the trick. Change your vocabulary. Instead of making exercise an obligation or duty, make it a necessity.

Changing that vocabulary with children puts a sense of urgency in your words that something is important and it is important now. Instead of saying, "You should do your homework before you go out," say "You must do your homework before you go out." There's a major difference there. Without a doubt, the homework will be done. Instead of saying, "You should eat your vegetables," say "You must eat your vegetables."

There is no room for uncertainty in the latter statement. The child does not have to think about whether to eat the vegetables and then make a decision. The decision has already been made by a wise parent.

As a parent, you may have some bad habits you think you should break. Should you give up smoking? I don't think that's a fair question. I think the real question is: Must you must stop smoking? How are you going to do it?

Consider the benefits, which include being more active with your child. That's not to mention the extra pocket change every week. Invest that money on improving your health instead of hastening your demise. I've heard many people say they should stop smoking, but very few succeeded unless they said "I must stop smoking." That affirmative rejection of smoking is exactly what's needed to mentally prepare for kicking the addiction. After all, Black Belt Parents have a responsibility to take care of themselves as well as their children.

> *"The future is purchased by the present."*
> Samuel Johnson

Take Control Of Your Life

Great communicators have the skill and expertise of a great mechanic. When a car comes into the shop, the great mechanic fiddles here and there and determines what is wrong. The great mechanic can see something, hear something, feel something or sense something that evades most of us. Great communicators work the same way. They are the people who seem to hold down a conversation effortlessly.

The man who earned the nickname the Great Communicator, former actor and President Ronald Reagan said, "There are no such things as limits to growth, because there are no limits on the human capacity for intelligence, imagination and wonder."

I went to the mall with one of my married friends to pick up a few things. Shawn was really upset about his five-year-old daughter, Cassandra. He could hardly believe someone so young could have such a stubborn mind of her own. She was constantly talking back to him and testing how far her rebellion could go. That morning, she reached his limit.

While he was getting dressed, Cassandra asked if she could have some soda. Shawn was in a hurry and shooed her away, but said he'd pour her a glass if she sat nicely and waited for him to finish dressing.

Well, Cassandra didn't want to wait. She walked out of the bedroom, right up to the refrigerator, opened the door and pulled out a 2-liter bottle of cola. She held the bottle in her arm as if she was holding a baby and unscrewed the cap. When she leaned over to put the cap on the counter, she tipped the bottle backwards, spilling soda on the floor. It splashed everywhere, including the ivory-colored dining room carpet. Shawn heard her gasp and ran out to see what happened. He yelled at her and gave her a time out. Cassandra just pouted. She wouldn't even apologize. As I mentioned, Shawn had had enough. He asked his mom to babysit and called me to go out. I could tell he was stressed and agreed to meet him. I picked him up and he barely sat in the car before he started going off on a rant.

"It's like she doesn't care. She can be so defiant. No matter what I say, she'll just stare at me like she doesn't even know what I'm saying. She has this vengeance," Shawn said. He continued rambling on until we pulled into the mall parking lot and started walking toward the department store entrance. That's when he stopped talking and froze in his tracks. I followed his gaze to the bumper sticker he was looking at and we both started laughing.

It read, "Mean people produce little mean people." Shawn clammed up and said, "Maybe she's a little more like her dad than I would like." I laughed and suggested ways he might be able to reach his daughter now that he identified what might be their common weak spot.

There Are More Last Minute Details Than There Are Last Minutes

There is a very fine line between what you can and cannot control. Find it and begin controlling what you can. Realize this: as much as your life is dedicated to this goal, you can not control your children. You can manage them and influence them, but they are out of your control. For a few blissful months at the beginning of life, you can control their movements. Even then, you still can't control what they do in place. And don't forget – change takes time. Your effectiveness as a parent and as a person is determined by your ability to plan for those things you can control and to leave room for change when there are things you can't control.

Effectiveness as a Black Belt Parent requires striking a balance between all the important facets of your life.

Chapter 6

Never Say No. See The Light

"The first requisite for success is to develop the ability to focus and apply your mental and physical energies upon the problem at hand without growing weary."

Thomas Edison

Thomas Edison invented the light bulb in 1879. In a stroke of genius, he put together all the elements to provide lasting light. That is, after years of research and about 2,000 failed attempts. In his previous efforts, he used many different kinds of gases, glass and threads. He sometimes made progress, but most of the time he was not even close to a solution.

"Just because something doesn't do what you planned it to do doesn't mean it's useless.... Results? Why, man, I have gotten lots of results! If I find 10,000 ways something won't work, I haven't failed. I am not discouraged, because every wrong attempt discarded is just one more step forward.... There are no rules here, we're just trying to accomplish something," he said.

Did Edison invent the light bulb in one day or several years? The correct answer is several years. All of the time and sweat he poured into his work materialized into something tangible in the course of one day. However, he never could have reached that accomplishment without learning about all the possible materials that could be used and trying each one. In fact, Edison relied on earlier discoveries to put together all the pieces that make lasting light. The invention of the light bulb was a collaborative effort of Edison's hard work.

"I never did anything worth doing entirely by accident... and none of my inventions came about totally by accident. They came about by hard work. Pretty much everything will come to him who hustles while he waits," Edison said.

After he succeeded with the light bulb, he continued to improve it. His work eventually gave rise to the electric industry. That's quite an accomplishment for someone who failed more than 2,000 times on a single project.

Don't ignore all of the success and knowledge you've gained from failure. If you learn from failure, you have valuable experience and that is a success. Failure should never be the last step in a process. If it is, then you have quit too soon and you really have failed. When you persevere, failure is just one of many steps on the road to success.

Success is the very last step. Thomas Edison failed many, many times until eventually he achieved success. If he had only tried 1,999 times, that would have been a failure. However, he recognized that each failure was not the end of the road, but one checkmark in the list of things to do before reaching success. If he had discovered what materials work early on in the process, perhaps he wouldn't have understood why it worked. He developed that knowledge over the course of his extensive research while building on the research of others.

This message is obvious when raising young children. When you first put a baby on a potty, do you expect him or her to use it right away? If not, do you give up? Of course not, you keep trying until the child succeeds. It would be silly to say, "That's it! You'll be in diapers the rest of your life!" Use that same persistence to achieve everything that you want done in your life.

In fact, use that same persistence on yourself. In many of your adult endeavors there is more at stake than soiled diapers. No matter what losses come from failure, pick yourself up and try again just as you'd expect a toddler to do. Knowing how to benefit from failure is a key to success.

Each Failure Is One Step Leading To Success

One eighth grade student, Danielle, wanted to go to a high school dance with her friend who was in tenth grade. Her mom said "no" because Danielle was too young to hang out with high school kids. In classic 14-year-old behavior, Danielle threw a fit as if her life would come to an end if she didn't go.

Danielle acted as if the world was coming to an end. She said that all of her friends were allowed to go to high school dances and they were no big deal and on and on. When her mom said she couldn't go, she wouldn't let up. She kept insisting and fighting with her. Danielle's mom did not give in and, boy, was Danielle angry. Her mom knew that as a parent, she must hold her ground firm and wait for the event to pass. She could also reject Danielle's demand while giving her hope she could get what she wanted in the future.

Danielle's mom was practicing Black Belt Parenting. A week later, I asked her how the situation was resolved.

"She still wishes she had been allowed to go and she's not happy, but at this point, Danielle's forgotten about it. It's funny how things change so quickly. The dance is history. Now, if she doesn't get her ears pierced, that will be the end of the world."

As a parent, you have the wisdom of time and experience on your side. You know what is right for your children and can make tough decisions for them. Remember that you were their age once. They have never been your age. Use some reverse psychology. Give them respect and a positive response, but stand firm on your rules. And since you must enforce the rules, the best way to say no is to say yes.

Just Say Yes

This may seem like peculiar advice, but it's always okay to say yes *as long as there is a contingency.*

In Danielle's case, Maryanne told her daughter, "Yes you can attend a high school dance – when you're in high school." Despite her daughter's temporary frustration, Maryanne hung in there and didn't give in. Her persistence matched and outlasted Danielle's persistence. In all cases, parents have the strength, motivation and power to outlast their children in these arguments. Use your power as parents to enforce the rules you think are important for nurturing your child. They will thank you in the end. Success is the very last step.

As Ann Landers wrote, "This, too, shall pass." But the lesson will endure. Deep down a good seed is planted. Your child knows what is okay and that it is your job to raise them so they don't grow up too fast or too slow.

Never say no to your children. That may seem like strange advice, but it is not as simple, nor as off base as it sounds. The answer to every yes/no question should start with yes and end with a condition for getting what the child wants. Black Belt Parents don't have to resort to an inflexible, conflict-building "no."

"Can I get a new dirt bike?"

"Yes, if you earn the money to pay for it."

"Can we stop for ice cream on the way home?"

"Yes, if you vacuum the living room when we get back.

"Will you raise my allowance?"

"Yes, if you raise your grades to straight A's."

"May I sleep over my friend's house tonight?"

"Yes, if I can talk to your friend's parents about it and you can guarantee you'll be home by 9 a.m."

Children can have anything they want, as long as they meet standards you set up. I offer the wisdom of Rabbi Neil Kurshan, in his book, <u>Raising Your Child To Be A Mensch.</u> "Teenage rebellion is a testing process in which young people try out various values in order to make them their own. But during those years of trial, error, and embarrassment, a child needs family standards to fall back on, reliable habits of thought and feelings that provide security and protection."

It's imperative for parents to insist that children do what they're supposed to do, when and how the parent expects it to be done. If a child skirts responsibility early in life, it becomes a natural reaction to obstacles in the future. Each time an excuse replaces responsibility, a brick is placed in the wall between the child and success.

There are times when children can get a special treat, or slightly break the rules without major consequences. That's part of life. However, the point here is to establish a habit or basic structure that children can follow so they know what's right, what's wrong, what's expected, and the potential outcome. Children look to you for guidance on what is correct behavior, what is normal, how they should respond in certain situations. Rebellion is a way they have of looking look to parents for guidance.

It is the job of a parent to watch that rebellion closely and rein it in whenever you deem it to be overreaching. Don't quit on your kids by letting them have their way. The challenges (and gray hairs) they bring will not be nearly as bad if the children stick to your basic rules.

There are some children who are more rebellious than others.

If a child wants to quit karate, but you know karate is good for him, your child may not respond to your nudging and positive insistence. That's no reason to give up. Quitting sets up the child for a lifetime of letting emotions get in the way of achievement. A healthy dose of persistence can be injected into every relationship. Persistence shows the child you are tough and that they need to learn toughness to hang in there with you. The stronger they are mentally, the better prepared they are for the challenges of life.

Insist that your child work hard on difficult tasks. Helping him or her with homework does not mean looking up the answers. It is rephrasing the question or asking a series of easier questions leading to discovery of the final answer.

I have a student, Kelly, who swore that she could not, no matter how hard she tried, do a shoulder roll. This move is similar to a forward roll, except your body rolls over your shoulder at an angle. If a student falls forward in a self-defense situation, he or she can go into a roll and pop back up rather than hit the ground. In a shoulder roll, the head doesn't touch the ground, so the move can be done anywhere, even on concrete. It's not complicated, but it requires practice until the motions come naturally. Kelly wasn't ready. Every time she tried, she would flop over onto her side in a half-roll or smack her head against the ground then push herself over. After the first five or six attempts, she didn't want to try anymore. Her head started to ache from hitting the ground and she said it felt awkward to try a shoulder roll. She was uncomfortable doing the move because she felt foolish when she went into it wrong then had to pull herself up from the mat instead of popping right up. She didn't want to do it anymore.

"I can't do it. My head hurts," Kelly told me.

"Okay, I understand you're frustrated. Take a break. Get a drink and stretch your muscles and then come back," I said.

After Kelly's three-minute break, she still resisted trying. I told her she didn't have an option. If she quit, her movements would always be limited by her mind's perception. A shoulder roll is not a back flip and it doesn't require a lot of physical ability. It's about maneuvering your body across the mat quickly and landing on your feet. I told Kelly the shoulder roll was a requirement and sent her to another area of the training mat to practice with another student, Matt.

Matt had mastered the shoulder roll earlier in the week, but he needed practice. I wanted Kelly to work with him so that between her attempts, she could see it executed the way it is supposed to be done. Matt was not resistant to doing shoulder rolls – to him, it was just practicing another move. Since doing too many shoulder rolls in a row can make you dizzy, I told them to run a lap in between each roll. Kelly sluggishly jogged around the mat after each attempt. Like clockwork, Matt did a shoulder roll, jumped up and started jogging. Then Kelly would throw her body towards her shoulder and somehow end up in a giant heap in the mat. She then pushed herself up and jogged around in a way that looked like she was dragging her feet as she bounced.

I have to admit Kelly wasn't able to do a shoulder roll by the end of the day. The next day she was looking forward to sparring instead of rolling. I had another idea in mind and insisted that Kelly try again. I told her that if she completed the roll, she could go back to sparring. I didn't want Kelly to give up, knowing that if she kept trying she would make it.

Her first efforts were way off the mark. I occasionally took a break from class to show her again and again how she could move her arm to do it. "Pretend someone is pulling your arm toward your waist and let your body follow your arm," I said. Well, that didn't work either. I tried again and it clicked. Kelly flipped around and she was so shocked that she made it in one move that she almost fell back down. A look of accomplishment washed over her face. There is no doubt that all those seemingly futile attempts were worth it because she got what she wanted. Kelly learned that by sticking to it, she could accomplish anything.

How many times did Kelly fail? Not as many as Thomas Edison, and he pressed on. You can give up only after you've tried at least 2,000 times. How's that for a great rule?

Waiting For Results

If you practice discipline and persistence now, the enjoyment and reward will come later. I had started teaching karate at the same time I started college. I knew that higher education would provide a better foundation for success. I desperately wanted to be the best karate instructor running the most successful business. That's not because of an overwhelming sense of competition, but of an overwhelming desire for success.

There were many sleepless nights and even more restless days when I wanted to give up. I wanted a college degree, but at times it didn't seem worth it. In my first semester, my grades were fair. The truth is, I never "accidentally" forgot to do my homework. I made that choice every single day. When I choose to be lazy today, I am also making the choice to fail my classes tomorrow.

When I saw my grades at the end of the semester, I resolved to be a better student, never wanting to feel the disappointment again of failing to meet my own expectations in class. I knew I had the ability to improve my average and it was up to me to stick to the goal of earning "B's" and "A's."

The next semester, I made vast improvements and got better grades because I earned them. It was the hardest time in my life, but the work paid off. I made the decision to work hard for four months with little immediate payback in exchange for the future benefits. That small sacrifice then helped make a big difference in me becoming a better businessman today.

I was able to reach my goals through hard work in college and in those start-up years of the first Action Karate. I enjoy my work and have accomplished a lot more than if I hadn't made the investment in a college education. Today, there are 17 Action Karate schools. Of course, hard work and responsibilities never end. But I have a great career built from a solid foundation set up early by being persistent in achieving goals.

Teach your children the important lesson of sticking it out even when a situation doesn't seem to go their way. If a child gets a poor grade on a chemistry test, it's not time to quit. It's time to suck it up and get back to hard work. When the situation is not the most advantageous, do what you have to do to get the job done.

Take the example of a student who was working on an essay for his history class. Karl was in ninth grade and the 10 page assignment was the most he ever had to write. His teacher gave the class one month to complete the assignment. Karl tried to get ahead of the schedule by working on it a few hours a week the first two weeks. He checked out a few books from the library and typed a few pages. On the Saturday before the assignment was due, Karl was typing away on his home computer when there was a sudden power outage. His house, along with 200 neighbors, was without power for two hours. Karl was furious. An afternoon's work was lost forever. He had plans to go out with friends the next day and told his mom he didn't have time to make up the work. He wanted her to call his teacher and explain what happened so that he could get out of the assignment. Mrs. Kaplan refused. Why? In real life, copping out is not an option.

If Mrs. Kaplan's computer fails, she can't call her boss and tell him she didn't get any work done because of a power failure. Mrs. Kaplan told Karl he had enough time to finish the report before it was due as long as he didn't go to the movies with his friends. It wasn't Karl's fault he was in that situation, but he had to adjust to the circumstances. Hey, that's life. Karl's Sunday was a boring day, but at least he finished his report and learned a valuable lesson.

One of my students broke his arm in a car accident three months before his black belt test. Eleven-year old Russell was stuck in a bad situation. He had two choices: earn his black belt on time by working harder or feel sorry for himself and wait until his arm healed. Russell's mom didn't give him that second choice. She is a believer in the idea that when life hands you lemons, make lemonade. Russell did a fine job of squeezing every drop of lemon juice out of his untimely injury.

During the next three months, Russell concentrated on kicks, stances and punching with his right arm only. For every limitation caused by his broken arm, there were twice as many routines he could practice instead. Russell even learned how to do a one-handed cartwheel. He could spin twice as fast in his spin kicks. He learned a new knee sweep that doesn't require using both hands.

When the cast came off one month before the test, Russell's left arm was weak and he had to strengthen it. All of the training to make up for the loss of his arm prepared Russell for the physical therapy and rehabilitation that followed. Russell's doctor marveled at how quickly he recuperated.

Before his arm fully recovered, it was time to qualify. At the test, he favored his right arm and had little use of one side of his body. That made the push-ups all the more difficult. Not even a broken arm will get you a free pass through a black belt test.

His performance relied on three-quarters of his limbs to perform, and they did. He overcompensated for his arm by showing off the new moves and making adjustments to techniques to use another form of defense. He passed with flying colors thanks to his persistence and the accident that opened up his abilities to a whole new level.

Not only that, Russell was very active at school and played a part in the school play. In his scene, robbers attack Russell. The script called for him to use his arms and the scene wouldn't make sense if Russell held back. He suggested to the teacher that he pretend to hurt his arm early in the scene so he was in too much pain to use it. It worked great! No one in the audience even noticed that the script had been changed. Russell took a bad situation and made it better. He showed great black belt attitude.

Giving It All

Successful people work through their fears and hesitations. Even when they don't feel up to giving 100 percent to a project, successful people do it anyway. Thinking about things you have to do and dreading them won't provide the motivation to get things done. This is best expressed in the simple philosophy: Don't put off until tomorrow what you can do today. Following that advice means that no matter how you feel, you will do what needs to be done.

Take action. If you don't feel like doing something, no amount of logic will likely motivate you. However, if you are getting work done, even work you don't feel like doing, the sense of accomplishment might put your emotions in a more positive light. Feelings won't change your action, but action will change your feeling. Don't let frustrations, disappointments or defeats set you back.

Down, Not Out

In the 2002 Olympics, an extraordinary drama unfolded in the last lap of the 1,000-meter short-track speed skating race. A pack of skaters collided a few feet before crossing the finish line. The favorite to win, American Apolo Anton Ohno, was among the skaters in that pack. His chances of getting the gold were slashed when he hit the ground as another skater who had been well behind the crash skated to gold. Ohno did not give up. He crawled across the finish line and captured the silver medal. Ohno could have easily stayed on the ice until the race ended, but he didn't give up. Even though he knew that the gold medal was already taken, he rebounded faster than the other skaters and still earned a coveted silver medal.

"I'm not shooting for No. 1. I'm just trying to give my best and walk off the ice with no regrets," said 19-year-old Ohno.

He has nothing to regret in that performance. He needed six stitches in his left thigh from a cut suffered in the fall. The silver medal isn't bad for a guy with six stitches who crawled over the finish line. In the same Olympic games, he went on to win the gold in another event.

That same persistence, determination and devotion to raising "gold medal" children is what separates Black Belt Parents from the also-rans.

Chapter 7

What Your Child Really Needs: Be A Parent, Not A Friend

Have you ever wondered how fishermen can bring themselves to work each day knowing the vulnerability of tiny vessels to the open seas? They spend months at a time riding the waves and navigating through some horrific storms in search of a good catch. It is one of the most dangerous professions in the world.

In many ways, parents have a lot in common with fishermen. Each sets out for the unknown, sensing storms and high seas just over the horizon. Each knows that the challenges ahead will be a true test of character and each challenge will be more difficult than the last. The specter of heartbreak or failure always looms large.

Yet, the lure of the open sea or the love of a child makes the risk worth the effort and sacrifice. It may be strange to think about raising a child in the terms of such danger and reward, but consider how much of your life is invested in your child.

You must commit an enormous amount of time and energy to your child. It's a daunting task and you'll be raising them right in a world of rough seas.

"A ship in harbor is safe - but that is not what ships are for."
John A. Shedd

If only you could keep your child in harbor for life—an impossible task for any parent. The only thing you can do is prepare your child while in harbor for the dangerous seas ahead. All parents want to protect their children from the scary pirates and other dangers lurking beyond their grasp.

Watching a child set sail into the world with well-known dangers is something you will have to accept. After all, your parents somehow managed to set you free. Help your children to pitch their sail on their own, so they will not be helpless in a wide-open sea where you can't protect them.

You may think you will always be around to keep your children safe, but you can't watch them all the time. Make sure they have all the tools to succeed on their own. There will come a time when you are far, far away and those lessons you taught will be important.

Your purpose in their life is to be a parent. Although you may be tempted to sugarcoat life to make it easier for them, take your responsibility seriously to teach them the facts of life – the good and bad. It is not your job to be a friend and hang out and let them do what they want. Once they hit the rough seas of the real world, there will be many people who aren't their friends. A positive upbringing with consistent discipline will give them the best opportunity to lead a successful life. That's the goal of <u>Black Belt Parenting</u>. Sometimes a child may want to quit something that becomes difficult.

Quitting is a learned behavior. The first time someone tries to quit something, it is part of the growing process and a child will try it to test limits. The second time someone wants to quit, it's okay to want to, it's just not acceptable to act on it. He or she has to be continuously conditioned not to give up after the first try. If quitting is accepted in the home, it becomes an option in life - throughout life and that can be a tragedy. I believe that it is possible to instill that message early in life and to nurture well-rounded, dedicated children who will not give in when the going gets tough.

Children must be strongly encouraged (motivated) to do things that are good for them, whether its homework, piano practice or eating their vegetables. You have a pretty good idea of what's good for your children. Sometimes it's tough to keep them on track when other responsibilities get in your way, but you must keep up with your children.

You have a wealth of knowledge and love to give them. When negative messages are mixed in, those gold nuggets you offer become covered in sand. Sift out the negativity that covers the real gold mine of advice that you have to offer. That could be a misplaced word, a negative message or just an angry or disap-pointed glance. It's dirt and it doesn't belong in the lives of your children.

You have every day to make a difference. When children learn how to quit, it is equivalent to handing them a lump of coal instead of a gold nugget. Make a commitment to give your child all the power he or she needs to go for the gold.

When children want something, one step has to be accomplished before they start to achieve that goal. They have to make a commitment. For example, when a child wants to join a little league baseball team, do you just sign him or her up? Of course not, the first thing you do is explain what is expected and that signing up is a commitment. It's not something that you do one day and drop the next. This builds confidence and discipline, which are two key principles of black belt excellence.

Parents must make their children go to school and take their medicine and brush their teeth – all of that is part of life. The principles you instill at a young age will follow them throughout life. They will then have the same skills, determination and diligence as the most successful people in the world.

Try this experiment. List the five most successful people in the world. They don't have to be the richest. They should be people who have accomplished great things. Take as much time as you like and then list them here.

1.

2.

3.

4.

5.

Black Belt Parenting

When you have all five names, think about what personality traits you believe makes them successful. What do they have that other people strive for? Are the same traits popping up for each person? There are patience, modesty, dedication tenacity, strength of mind, strength of character, courtesy, intelligence, action and so many more. Most likely a few words applied to each person. There's a very good reason for that: Those are the ingredients for success.

Notice that the word action made my list. I hope it was on yours. That's what children really need. Dish it out heaping spoonfuls so they can cook up successful futures and pass on the magic ingredient to their own children.

It is simply not fair to let children make decisions that will affect their lives negatively when they are not prepared to make those decisions.

Parents do not have to force being friends with their children. That happens naturally when you practice Black Belt Parenting. Once they grow past the stage when the parent is responsible for making their decisions, the bonding will be in place. Friendship can grow. It is much more crucial that a parent play the role of disciplinarian than friend. Let their peers be their friends. Their peers certainly aren't going to take on the role of disciplinarian, so who else is left to handle that all-important chore?

A student who doesn't have proper support from parents can

be truly handicapped when he or she enters the world. One of my students, Hector, was excellent and a really tough competitor. Unfortunately he had a character flaw keeping him from being one of the best: a behavior handicap. He didn't work well with other students. He was demanding and rude to instructors. He was greedy, arrogant and always insisting on having his way. When he scored a point or won a sparring match, he would be a bad winner and laugh at his opponent. When an opponent scored on him, he would swear that he wasn't actually hit and get angry that the judges would score a point against him. He made up all kinds of excuses as to why he was losing. Hector didn't win any friends and the instructors did not tolerate his behavior. So why was Hector such a holy terror?

Hector was constantly misbehaving because that had become acceptable. The 11-year-old wasn't to blame. He was never taught how to be a grateful winner or a gracious loser. He was spoiled. Hector always got what he wanted. He would throw a temper tantrum to force his parents to comply with his wishes. And the tactic worked. What other type of behavior would you expect from an 11-year old given those circumstances?

Hector's parents were too busy trying to be his friend to ever say no. He was never disciplined. When asked about this, his father said, "I want Hector to have everything he wants. I don't want him to get upset. If I can afford to give him something, then he can have it."

This left the rest of society to say no to Hector.

In school, Hector was one of the last children chosen for team games in the schoolyard. He had few friends. In karate class, instructors were especially tough on him because they knew he wouldn't work hard unless constantly pressed to keep trying.

Parents want their children to be happy and healthy with no limitations. Never using the word no gives your child a handicap that will make it harder for him or her to succeed in life. Refusing to discipline your child is giving him or her added challenges. Success requires much more effort to compensate for the handicap. Considering the way Hector was raised, his parents gave their son a serious handicap. He can't fit in with other children as easily and succeeding in life will be more challenging. No one will want to befriend, date, hire or live with such a selfish person.

Granted, most parents don't want to say no to their child, but forgoing discipline is no road to happiness or fulfillment. Parenting is a grand struggle between giving to your child and instituting discipline. It is important for you to think about how you want to balance those responsibilities. The center line may be different for each parent. There may be days or weeks or months when the balance is off. Keep reevaluating what needs to be done and take steps to reestablish and maintain that balance.

Ask The Question

In a 2001 anti-drug campaign, a series of adults made emphatic statements about their children such as, "I know my daughter doesn't do drugs. I know because I ask all the time."

How else will you know? You're the parent. It is your job to intrude on their lives and watch everything they do. They are your responsibility and your child's well-being is the most important thing in your life. Teenagers may not want to answer you, but they can't avoid talking if you ask the question. It is your job to ask. Know who your child's friends are, where they hang out and what they do. Children will make their own breathing room and they always test their boundaries. You must stay on top of those boundaries and make sure they don't stretch beyond the limits you set. Keep an eye on your children even when they resist it. In the end, they'll thank you. And that's what matters.

Here's the scary part: the only way you're going to know you did a good job is to wait for their development through the years. You can't be totally confident that you raised your kid right until they start making good decisions on their own - and they don't do that until they are out of your control. Nagging and snooping can put a wall between you and your child. Asking questions is the best way to find out what your child is doing.

Who are your children? Can you tell me their likes and dislikes? What are their goals? You can't get away with a guess.

You have to go beyond some half understood explanation and come up with accurate answers. Get involved. Sure, it will take a lifetime to see the outcome.

Take a few minutes to write down some things you think are important to know about your child. Keep track to find out if the child's best friend, taste in music, hair style or sleep schedule changes. Pay attention to details. If you don't know how your children are developing, they will change before your very eyes and you may not be able to trace or understand the changes. Adapt to the changes in your child's life and take special notes of anything drastic that happens. It is okay to suspect your child is doing something wrong - drinking, doing drugs or doing something illegal. It is not okay to ignore those suspicions. If you have an effective system of discipline, it will be difficult for the child to lie convincingly. If you are armed with information, there will be no room for lies.

There is a common saying: No one can hurt you unless you let them. This is true, as is: Your kids can't break your rules without your permission. You are the boss, the example, the role model. If the rules aren't enforced it's because you didn't enforce them and it is your children who will pay the heaviest price.

Be Consistent

Don't create high standards for your child one day, only to relax all of them the next. This creates confusion over why the standards are there in the first place and it will gradually make it harder to convince your child he or she is important over time. This isn't the same as allowing your child to have ice cream one day and not the next. That is a schedule. However, allowing your child to have ice cream for all three meals the next day is a complete abandonment of your standards.

Black Belt Parents are consistent in their discipline. Do not allow your children to talk back to you. Such behavior undermines your authority for the moment and robs your ability to guide them in the long-term. When children are permitted to talk back, the person who makes all the rules loses some of his or her authority. This takes away the ability to guide children in other areas.

Children attain a sense of security through discipline. They want the freedom to experiment with life, but mom and dad have to let them know when something is wrong. When the child can't turn to mom or dad for that sense of security the line between right and wrong is blurred. Children who get everything they want aren't taught the difference between right and wrong so they pursue both. This is a difficult way to approach life because other people, such as teachers and peers, just won't tolerate that type of behavior. The child will pay a lifelong penalty.

Until children are adults they are not your equal. They do not have equal say in decision making. If you become a pal to your child, you give up some of your parenting authority. Draw a clear line: you are the adult, they are the child. If a friend tells you to do something, does it have the same weight as your boss instructing you? Of course not. You regard that person differently. You see your boss as an authority figure and you have to follow his or her rules. You see a friend as someone offering advice – advice you can choose to take or ignore. Is that how you want your child to perceive your relationship?

Discipline is not a bad word. It is not a negative force. Discipline is not about instilling fear in your children. Children will follow your directions based on respect and trust if the discipline is positive. If the discipline is negative, they very well may respond to their fear. Another word that can be used for discipline is guidance. Disciplining your child is giving them guidance for how to behave in the real world. It is also a kind of education. They will learn from your influence. Discipline is a way of teaching them what is right and wrong and what values are most important in life. Unfortunately, failing to institute any consistent discipline is also teaching them. Both parents need to agree on and be actively involved in the child's discipline.

If one parent is lax about punishing the child, the child will likely walk all over that parent and see mom or dad as an easy way out of any given situation. At the same time, the same child will have all the respect and confidence in the other parent. As much as children hate to hear it, discipline is a sign of love. "I'm only punishing you to show that I love you." While that isn't comforting when the child is on a time out, or grounded, it speaks the truth.

What are the benefits of having a disciplined child? They are compassionate to others, have good manners, and are eager to do well. They are willing to work for what they want and realize that discipline aids in earning things in life, whether those things are good grades, a great job or a nice car. A disciplined person learns to do what needs to be done to accomplish specific goals. The only way to teach children discipline is to set up, explain and live by clear guidelines. Every parent has the power and resources to provide that for their child. The lessons you teach your child from the heart outweigh any presents or money you can give. Money does not buy happiness. The television news is flooded with people who have more money and fame than most of us dream about, but they are chronically unhappy and unfulfilled. Money can't do for you what discipline and appreciation can.

Discipline must start at an early age. Even before a child is old enough to do chores, parents naturally take to making sure the toddler starting to walk doesn't go down stairs, touch a hot light bulb, knock over chairs or poke someone in the eye. Those are the days when discipline is simple because you can easily control a child's every move and watch him or her at all times. If need be, you can physically stop your child from whatever potentially harmful act they're about to do.

When children are old enough to push a vacuum, sweep the floor or fold their own clothes, let them. Tell them they are doing a wonderful job, even though the 5-year-old is really spreading the crumbs all over the floor. You can always follow up afterward and clean the mess. The point here is to give them confidence doing chores early on and to make it something they want to learn how to do. There is no reason to fold your five-year-old's clothes if he or she is perfectly content folding them crookedly and putting them in the drawer that way. Maybe later when you're child isn't home, you can arrange things more neatly. It's okay if the clothes aren't folded perfect. The child at that age feels a real sense of accomplishment for doing those tasks without help, even if they're not done right. Continuing practice will bring about the necessary skills.

"Our challenge as parents is to be patient enough to allow our children to take 10 minutes to do something that would take us a few seconds," wrote Stephanie Martsen, a family therapist, in The Magic of Encouragement. Matsen encourages parents to allow children to develop what she calls their 'struggle muscle,' which — like any other muscle — is developed through regular exercise.

What a great way to sum up your child's early attempts: they're flexing their struggle muscle.

It won't seem as much of a chore when they're older if

they're used to doing it. You won't be viewed as the only person who is supposed to do these things. If a child is never asked to do something, he or she naturally views that chore as a parent's responsibility. The chores are small efforts that will erase the need for as much discipline in the future. When children are doing their own laundry and cleaning up after themselves, you will see the effect of your disciplinary efforts.

When children do something wrong, they very often know they weren't supposed to do it and expect to be punished. If they get away with it without their parents finding out, they feel guilty. What happens when you do find out about something the child did, but then don't punish the act? Their sense of guilt dissipates. If this happens a few times, the child doesn't feel guilty any more over breaking the rules and the infraction becomes a habit.

My friend tells a great story on how he learned a lesson about stealing. When he was eight, he wanted strawberry ice cream but his mom said he couldn't have any. He was brooding when he looked in his parent's bedroom and saw three dollars. He took the money and ran to the corner store and bought his own ice cream. He went to a makeshift tree house in his back yard to eat the stolen goods and the first few spoonfuls were absolutely delicious. But the boy realized he couldn't store his ice cream because it would melt. So he did what any eight year old would do. He ate the entire half-gallon. Not surprisingly, he got sick. When his mom saw what he had done, she refused to cater to his stomachache. She just left him to take care of himself. He spent three hours crouching in front of the toilet without a single word from his mom. She let him suffer the consequences of his action. To this day, he has not stolen a cent. He hasn't touched strawberry ice cream either! His mom's strategy gave him an eye-opening experience taught him a lesson that runs deeper in his mind than the desire for ice cream.

Don't worry about whether your kids like you. If you need someone to like you all the time, buy a dog. This is not a negotiable point in Black Belt Parenting. If your children get angry when you punish them, that's okay. It's a normal reaction. You don't need to assuage their anger or take back the punishment. A misbehaving child needs punishment and it can not come from a friend. Every child needs a responsible adult to guide him (or her) and tell him what is right and what is wrong.

Chapter 8

How To Handle Crying Kids

Children cry indiscriminately. Like adults, they cry when they're sad, angry, hurt or embarrassed, but also when they're tired, dissatisfied, sleepy, bored, sick, hungry or happy. Crying helps get them what they want. Don't coddle children if they are old enough to understand why they are crying if that reason is to manipulate a situation. You're just sending the message that turning on the tears is an effective tool for the child to get his or her way.

I had just such a student in a beginner class. Whenever Scott didn't want to do an exercise he would run off the exercise mat and cry to his mother. She would hold him and tell him he didn't have to go back, but a few minutes later, he'd timidly step back onto the mat and rejoin class. The truth is that he would get frustrated when he didn't do as well as he envisioned. He saw other students around him with more experience executing the moves faster and stronger, so he'd cry his way out of the situation.

Allowing such behavior to continue would have only made matters worse. If he were to stay on the mat and practice, he would be able to kick higher and punch faster and soon others would look up to him. With some encouragement, mom agreed to stay out of sight during class. Scott had nowhere to run. The next time he started to cry, no one coddled him. In fact, we ignored the crying and complimented his kicks. Within a few seconds he wiped away the tears and channeled his frustration into the karate. He never ran to his mom during class again.

A good strategy for dealing with crying kids is to distract them from the cause of their discouragement.

Here's a perfect example. One of my classes was playing a game similar to touch football. Byron was running with the ball toward a teammate when he inadvertently ran into a taller and much bigger player from the opposing team. A collective gasp fell over the parents when they saw Byron and the taller boy collide. There was a loud thud and the ball dropped from Byron's hands. A few silent seconds elapsed and Byron started to wail.

The game halted and everyone stared as Byron stood in the middle of the floor bawling. I immediately pulled him to the corner of the room so that he was facing the back wall instead of everyone else. I asked him what he had for breakfast. He was so startled by such a strange question that he stopped crying and mumbled, "Cheerios." I asked a few more questions such as how many bowls of Cheerios and so on. Pretty soon, Byron was ready to rejoin his team. Why did he stop crying? Because he forgot why he was upset in the first place. Byron wasn't really hurt. He was ashamed that he dropped the ball, embarrassed that a bigger kid ran into him and scared when he realized everyone was watching. By taking his mind off of that and making him realize, without even knowing it, there was no reason to be embarrassed, Byron was able to overcome his fear.

When Byron's mother saw the collision, she was ready to run onto the mat and ask the typical questions, "Are you hurt? Do you want to leave?" Since Byron was embarrassed, he likely would have exaggerated his injuries and asked to leave.

Later, she asked me what I had said to give Byron so much confidence. I recommended trying a wonderful strategy the next time he cried. "First, see if he is injured. Then distract him from the injury. Encourage him to stand up and move around on his own and ask him questions while he does it. That way he won't be concentrating on being embarrassed. He'll be busy thinking about other things and once he realizes he's stopped crying, it will be too late to start up again."

Byron's mother adopted these strategies until they were no longer necessary. Byron stopped crying when he was embarrassed because he knew if he wasn't hurt he could get right back in the game and people would think him a tough competitor. Now Byron is one of the most outgoing kids in class.

Chapter 9

Quitters Never Win

"My great concern is not whether you have failed, but whether you are content with your failure."

Abraham Lincoln

Remember, when children fail and want to give up, it is because of a temporary setback. If something didn't work out the first time they tried, children might be discouraged from trying again. They may feel a sense of failure.

"Failure is an event, never a person," said William D. Brown. Let your children know that just because they didn't achieve something on the first attempt, they are not failures. Don't let them believe that for a second or it will become a self-fulfilling prophecy.

When children lose enthusiasm for something, it may be because they feel they aren't talented enough. They fall off the horse a few times and don't want to get back on because they're afraid of falling. It is important to send the message that falling behind occasionally is okay. Staying back there is not acceptable.

"You don't drown by falling in the water; you drown by staying there."

Edwin Louis Cole

Motivational Stories

"Our deepest fear is not that we are inadequate. Our deepest fear is that we are powerful beyond measure. It is our light not our darkness that frightens us." said Nelson Mandela.

Think about that quote as it applies to parenting. The power to control someone else's life can be a frightening thought. *The goal of being a parent is to take that overwhelming power and influence in a child's life and give him or her happiness and a foundation to pursue dreams.* There is no doubt that you can bring joy into a child's life. Don't be afraid to use that power and take the child to task whenever necessary. There is nothing more important in a child's life than its parents. It is a wonderful and daunting power.

Children, and adults, have a tendency to go after their dreams and interests with fervor. A child who wants to learn to play the guitar may ask on a daily basis for guitar lessons, never letting up. The child may strum away at the toy guitar for hours a day until ready for a real one. When something peaks our interest, it's only natural to spend our spare time pursuing it. As an adult, you may have decided higher education or volunteering at a local community organization is important. These are things that piqued your interest and you committed to them at a time when you were completely enthused by the thought.

However, a few weeks later when that first major assignment is due, your enthusiasm may have waned. When your friends are planning a weekend trip to the beach, you may regret that you agreed to help your civic club clean the creek on Saturdays. These obligations started to feel like a burden and you may have been searching for a "Get out of jail free" pass to avoid your responsibilities. But you didn't give up. You took responsibility seriously because you know that you made the commitment because those things are important and they make you a better person in the long run.

All children go through phases in developing their personality and how they want to spend their time. There are times when their responsibilities catch up with them and they want to quit. These are the occasions when a parent's influence is crucial to insist they stick to it. Black Belt Parents reinforce the benefits of commitment, not becoming a quitter, and the importance of sticking to a goal until you see it through.

"Well done is better than well said."
Benjamin Franklin

When You Lose Enthusiasm

I am duplicating two letters from the Dear Abby advice column. These are wonderful success stories of parents teaching their children important life lessons at a time when the child wanted to quit.

Dear Abby,

Your advice to force children to practice was right on the

mark. Most children hate to practice, and our son and daughter were no exceptions. My husband got tired of all the fighting and said "Let them quit - it's too much of a hassle." I said "Over my dead body!" After that, there were few arguments. Today, our daughter Marylow Churchill, sits principal second violin in the Boston Symphony, and our son Paul, studied cello at Julliard.

Dear Abby,

I'm a mother who forced her kids to practice. Why not? It was for their own good. We force our kids to take baths, brush their teeth and eat their vegetables, turn off the TV and do their homework, don't we? My son wanted to quit piano when he was 10. I said "No way - you are not quitting!" I knew that my judgment was better than a child's. Today he is a conductor and professor at the Cincinnati Conservatory of music.

I am so proud of the efforts those parents made to insist their children exceed their expectations and reach levels most people only dream of. I have so many examples of students in my class who almost gave up then turned their attitude around. Here's one.

Twelve-year-old Matt wanted to drop out of karate and his parents wouldn't let him. At 14, he earned his black belt. At 15, he was winning trophies at national tournaments and still attending class twice a week, even when he was sick. At 16, he earned his license and started driving to class himself. He was here five days a week and his progress at this time was extraordinary. At 17, he told me his dream was to run a karate school. I told him that he was well prepared to take on that responsibility, but first he had one major assignment. He has to thank his parents.

At first, Matt only thought about how he and I had worked together training all those years. He had almost forgotten the times his parents drove him to class, in the rain and snow, and how they gave up their afternoons to drive him to tests, class, special training sessions, pick up his new uniform, and take him to tournaments. He forgot that when he wanted to quit, they didn't allow it. Matt benefited from all these things that had nothing to do with how I worked with him. Instead of just saying thank you, he wrote a letter to express how he felt.

Dear Mom and Dad,

    I am writing this letter because I wanted to tell you how I feel. I wanted to write it down so that I would find the right words.

    When you grounded me for skipping school that time and I couldn't go to the Eagles game, I told you I hated you.

    When our car broke down and we had to ride in a junky station wagon, I was embarrassed to go anywhere with you.

    When you wouldn't let me quit karate and soccer, I

resented you.

When you nagged me about who I was hanging out with and embarrassed me in front of my friends, I told you I wished you would stay out of my life. And now that I have realized my dream with a black belt, I can look back at those times and realize that you did what's best for me. Thank you for grounding me. Thank you for driving me around. Thank you for making me stick to it. And, yes, thank you for nagging me.

I dedicate this to you.

Love, Matt.

Matt's parents deserve an award for their successful son.

When you finish reading <u>Black Belt Parenting</u>, don't just talk about how you are going to encourage your children to stick to their dreams. Take action. Don't let your children make promises they don't keep.

When I started writing this book, I read books and sought advice from many people, including notable motivational speakers and parenting experts from around the nation. I thought of how my own parents raised me and the lessons I learned from friends. But I kept coming back to one source of knowledge that really makes up the backbone of this book: my students.

Every day when I teach karate, I spend time with a group of wonderful children and adults who are the case studies for this book. They have taught me how to treat people and how to create a positive atmosphere. How have they taught me this? By sticking to their goals with a positive attitude. By achieving black belt excellence. By showing up for class. By being good, and then great, at what they do. Our greatest teachers here at Action Karate have been the students we work with on a daily basis. They show us that our work is worthwhile and they want for themselves the same thing we want for them.

My most concrete proof of the success of this program comes twice a year when the advanced students prepare for their black belt test. The preceding months define the character of the people who stick to the program. These students are edging toward the toughest test of their training, Black Belt Boot Camp. This is an intensive workout and testing over several hours that turns boys, girls, men and women into Black Belts. It is when all of the training comes together in a physical, emotional grueling day of showing what they can do and what they know. It is no small feat.

As part of the requirement to enter the testing, black belt candidates have to write essays explaining why they want to go through the effort and what that effort means. This helps me gain the understanding that the lessons we've stressed over the years of training have sunk in and they are learning karate for the right reasons. The essays also give them personal insight by putting something they believe into words. They gain perspective by writing then reading how they feel and it brings them closer to the goal.

These essays are touching, inspirational, tough-as-nails and humbling. I would recommend that every one write out their goals for everything they do. This will keep the goals fresh and simply explain why you do what you do.

The essays I've included at the end of this chapter represent a sample of those who have come through the doors of Action Karate, who have worked through the challenges in life and are some of the greatest people I have ever met. The message can sink in at any age. Some black belts are as young as 10 years old. The youngest Black Belt is included in the essays and he wrote the essay on his own.

And you can teach an old dog new tricks. The oldest person I ever granted a Black Belt is 82- year-old Dave Hart. The Harley-riding octogenarian could do more push-ups than many younger students and exuded the Black Belt attitude.

Within these essays, many common themes emerge that touch on many of the issues I stress in this book. I hope they serve as proof to you that living your life with a Black Belt attitude, raising Black Belt kids and teaching the Black Belt Parenting is a worthwhile pursuit that leaves everyone who had a part in it with a greater sense of pride and self-worth.

The Essays

"My black belt means I have guts. I am not afraid to go beyond the limits. I have built up the strength in my body. I

have increased the knowledge in my mind. I have kept the honesty in my heart...

"I have faith in myself. Getting my black belt will mean I have worked very hard meeting the goals that I have set. I am a good student. I think my teachers are the greatest because they are extremely good in martial arts. They teach us that karate is only to defend yourself.

"When I get my junior black belt, I will fell very good. My parents will be proud and happy for me. Life is not one big step, it is a bunch of little steps."

David

★★★

"I've attended Action Karate for five years and I've always enjoyed it. I will be attending Black Belt Boot Camp so that I will be able to earn my Junior Black Belt. It really means much to me to have the privilege that some kids don't have to go to karate, to learn and have teachers to teach us self control, discipline, the right attitude and other things. I am appreciative that I have the opportunity that I can go to karate and a mother who wants me to go to karate.

"I can hardly wait until the day when I come home from Black Belt Boot Camp. I will celebrate at my house and have a big party if my mom says we can have a party with all my friends, family, aunts and uncles."

Shaina Marie

★★★

"Being a member of the Black Belt Club means setting your goal high and meeting all the challenges in obtaining it. When I first walked into Action Karate and witnessed the classes I knew it was the right studio for me and my children. The unique teaching style is awesome and lends itself to a complete dedication to personal growth.

"Before I came to Action Karate I couldn't figure out why I always had the best of intentions but nothing ever worked out for me. I rarely ever reached my full potential. In coming to Action Karate and hearing such positive philosophy it has opened my eyes to what it takes to be a success –making my goals clear and specific. "Besides the positive atmosphere and philosophy, it is an honor to train with other Black Belt Club members who have also committed themselves to such a challenge. Together we work and sweat, talk and laugh and genuinely cheer each other's efforts. For OUR goals are high: knowledge in the mind; knowledge is power, the power you need to achieve your goals. Honesty in the heart; being true to yourself in what you feel. This will enable you to grow. Strength in the body; this comes from a good balanced training of body and mind. This will keep you focused. Our goals here are specific.

"At Action Karate you will achieve all this and more. Its right in front of you-grab it. The sky is the limit. So reach for the stars. ASAH!"

Brian

★★★

"When I started as a white belt I thought it was just fun to do. When moved on to each higher belt I could feel more confident and stronger. Sometimes when I didn't feel like going to karate my mom would say, "Let's go. You can do it." We would go and once I was in class I was really glad I'd come. Sometimes the new techniques seemed so hard and then after lots of practice they seemed easier and I wanted to learn more. Becoming a Junior black belt would be the reward for all the hard work."

Ryan

★★★

"Being a junior black belt is important to me because achieving this rank shows I have the discipline necessary to reach my goals in life. A goal of mine is to develop my swimming to be able to make my high school and college teams. This will take years of hard work and practice. Being a junior black belt shows I have the discipline to do this. Karate has given me the courage to do the right thing. As I grow up people will ask me to do things that are wrong that will hurt my mind and body. Achieving black belt has given me the courage to do the right thing even when it is not popular.

"Achieving junior black belt has taught me never to quit. School, swimming, karate and other things can be hard at times. It would be easy to quit. When I think of quitting I remember

student creed number one and never quit. Karate has helped me develop a positive attitude. Achieving junior black belt shows everyone I have a positive attitude.

Junior black belt has been my first major goal in life. This has set a high standard for the rest of my life."

James

★★★

"Along my journey to receive my black belt I felt I grew in many ways. I am now wiser with more self-control. The self-control helps me focus more in school and at home. Therefore it helped me get wiser. It helped me think of what is happening in my life and what I am doing. I also grew physically stronger. I worked hard at every week and feel as though it paid off.

"A black belt means I have done well. It means I have put a lot of effort into my karate. I have seen friends of mine receive their black belt before me and I have been inspired from that.

"I want my black belt because I love karate and I will not let anything interfere with that. I want to practice karate for the rest of my life, and Action Karate is the best choice I ever made."

Victor

★★★

"In these past three years, I have had more self-control, discipline, confidence and strength. I am also proud to have the talent of karate and the ability to earn my black belt.

"I have learned from all of my mistakes. The most important thing is reaching my goal. I have always wanted my black belt. Now it is time to set a new goal. I am not sure what my next goal is going to be, but I know it is going to be a great one.

"I have also enjoyed assisting the lower belts and I am looking forward to doing it again. Assisting the three and four year olds has helped me gain self-control."

Dennis

★★★

"After all the hard work that I have done I finally achieved my goal and will soon start a new level of my black belt. I would now have to set new goals and learn new techniques and I also know that I would have to work twice as hard and that step by step I will journey to understanding, admiration and will wear the most prestigious excellent recognized symbol which is my Black Belt. Once I obtain this next level "triumphantly" I know anything is possible as long as I put my mind in to it."

Ingrid

★★★

"Total focus, concentration, dedication and a pure desire are all necessary on the road to becoming a black belt. There are many reasons I would like to receive the prestigious honor of black belt. I intend to finish what I start and the reward in this situation is a black belt."

"Point number one: Dedication."

"In the past few months, I have discovered a greater ability to concentrate which I attribute to martial arts. I can read and recollect most of the material for some time afterward; A problem I have been bouting with since I was a child. It is hard to congest the pain to a tolerable level so that I can focus without frustration."

"Point number two: Focus and concentration."

"Constant testing of my abilities has brought me here with the will to succeed. I train until I am in pools of sweat. I push myself beyond the physical limit ... until I can control my actions with my mind. My mind is set, I will stop at nothing to become a black belt. Whether it be recovering from injury, picking up after falling down or just simple physical exhaustion, I will complete my desire ... the nearly inhuman passion, to become a black belt."

Peter

Do these children sound like quitters to you? Of course not. I hope you are as inspired by their words as I am. We can learn a lot from those we teach. After all, helping children achieve their hopes, dreams and lofty goals is what Black Belt Parenting is all about.

Chapter 10

Three Kick-Butt Words: I Love You

"Love does not begin and end the way we seem to think it does. Love is a battle, love is a war; love is a growing up."

Jaesaldin

We have many ways to say I love you.

With a kiss, a hug, a pat on the back, high five, smile or a look.

A small favor or sacrifice.

Or we can just say it.

Aloha I'a Au Oe in Hawaiian.

Te amo in Spanish.

Chit pa de in Burmese.

Je t'adore in French.

Ich liebe Dich in German.

Ti voglio bene in Italian.

Aheri in Luo, the language in Swahili.

Iyay Ovlay Ouyay in Pig Latin.

Ndinokuda in Shona, the language in Shona.

Ya te volim in Yugoslavian.

Mahn doostaht doh-rahm in Iranian.

Mujhe Tumse Muhabbat Hai in Urdi.

Tora dost daram in Persian.

Techihhila in Sioux.

Lubim ta in Slovak.

Whatever language you speak, make sure your children know that you mean it. Saying those words over and over again is very important. Those are the three magic words to live by, to get you through the hard times and to get your children through the hurdles in life.

When I talk to people who don't realize the influence of those three words, I tell the story of Raymond, whose parents never said "I love you." He was a bitter man who had a hard time staying in relationships and frequently blamed his problems on the fact that his parents did not say those three words to him.

When Raymond was 26, his mother went into a coma. As he sat by her hospital bed, Raymond told his mother he loved her, but, of course, she couldn't respond. She died two days later. Raymond was torn up that she died without saying I love you.

When his father became gravely ill with cancer four years later, Raymond worked up the courage to confront him about the lack of love. Raymond decided he wanted to resolve the guilt and questioning once and for all. He visited his father, having realized this was his last chance to find out why he hadn't heard those three words growing up. His dad, with a tear in his eye, said simply, "Of course I love you. I thought you knew."

Raymond's parents could have saved him much anguish in life if they had only spoken their feelings. They were not bad parents. They treated him well and gave him the tools he needed to become a successful real estate agent. Without hearing that he was loved, though, he was held back from true happiness.

"Looking back, I have this to regret, that too often when I loved, I did not say so," he said.

You will never regret saying I love you. Even when your child is a teenager, keep saying it. They may not respond or seem to care that you're saying it, but I love you are powerful words that stick on the inside.

When children don't hear those words, they can be disturbed about it for life, always questioning whether they are capable of love. There are two challenges to loving your children:

✦ Saying I love you.

✦ Showing I love you.

These takes patience, time and unfaltering dedication and sacrifice.

"Love has nothing to do with what you are expecting to get, it's what you are expected to give - which is everything."

Anonymous

Spend Time With Your Children

You can't simply find the time to be with your children. You must make time and put it on the top of your priorities list. Many parents, especially working mothers, feel guilty about being away from their kids. Well, it is true that nothing can replace spending time with your children, however, balancing a life and career is not selfish. What's important is the quality of the time you spend with your kids, not so much the quantity.

When you are with your children, give them all of your attention. It is a good idea to occasionally push another responsibility off your schedule just to let them know your priorities stand with them.

Make no mistake, though. You don't have to feel obligated to do this all the time. Children have perfected the guilt trip to an art. Don't fall for it. If you are busy and need time to take care of other responsibilities, don't let your kids down by telling them how important your other responsibilities are. They will feel like they are not as important and will feel the need to compete for your attention.

Never say, "I want to play with you, but I have to work." Address this situation by setting a finite limit to the time you spend with them so they have specific expectations. If your time is limited and a child wants to play a game, make it a game that has a relatively quick end. Perhaps if you play soccer, the game will end when someone scores a point.

As soon as this strategy affords you a healthy balance between work and family, the child will find a new way to push your buttons. That's what they do. Your children might try their hand at the art of negotiation. This is where playtime can be heart-wrenching.

Valerie learned this when she played a game with her four-year-old son Devin. She is a sales assistant who occasionally works from her home so that she can be with her son. Devin spends three days a week in day care and Valerie or her husband is home the rest of the time. Devin knows working from home is part of mom's routine. You never know how children will adjust to their environment and Devin, in his four-year-old wisdom, caught on to his mom's strategy to keep their games short. Instead of settling for one point when they played soccer, he started prodding for more.

"Please can we play to five points?" asked Devin.

"Professional soccer games don't usually go up to five points. Let's play for one point. Besides I don't want to lose by that many points," Valerie said.

"Please, please, please," Devin continued. "How about four points?"

"How about three and you have a deal," Valerie said.

Devin smiled at his successful negotiations and made the deal. It is okay to negotiate with your children to give in a little. Make sure you hold back, though, so that you aren't completely giving in to everything they want.

When you spend time with your kids, make sure they know they have all of your attention. Running around to fold the laundry and answer the phone lets them know you are distracted. Since you are a busy person, it will serve your purpose to make that quality time so you aren't scrambling to make up for it later. Answer the phone after the game is over, or after you are finished helping with homework. Or better yet, make the chores part of a game. If you include the child in doing the laundry, it saves you some of the effort and the child gets to spend more time playing with you.

Your time is precious. Whatever you are doing at one particular moment has to be your most important task and deserves all of your attention. Otherwise, you will have to work harder later to make up for those distractions.

At the moment you are working with your child to explain the homework assignment, give it your full attention. When you are writing an important report to a client, give it your full attention. Each task will be completed with higher quality without taking a higher quantity of time.

Do you find yourself having elongated family disputes or mundane discussions during work time? Imagine spending the afternoon preparing a highly technical report on a new product your company is offering. Then the phone rings.

"Hi, mom. What's for dinner?"

"I'm planning to make spaghetti."

"We don't have any sauce."

"Okay, then I'll pick it up on my way home from work. Did you take out the trash?"

"No. It will be done before you get here. Hey, there's a class field trip in two weeks to the chocolate factory. Can you be a chaperone?"

"I don't know. I'll check my schedule. Remember to take the trash out. I'll talk to you later."

Now instead of concentrating on your technical report, you are thinking:

1) Remember to buy sauce.

2) Check if the trash is taken out.

3) Prepare for a field trip and check the schedule.

That divided focus is fair neither to your company, nor to your family. It is best to save these conversations for when you get home. Plan your meals for the week and make time when you get home to discuss the day's and the next day's activities with your children. This will make you a better employee because you aren't sharing your mind with your home activities. This also forces you to be prepared and avoid unnecessary trips to the supermarket or other time-consuming chores which will take away from your quality time with the children, so they won't feel short-changed.

Of course, kids can be impatient and want immediate attention. At those times firmly let them know you would love to spend every second with them and suggest something else for them to do. "I would love to play monopoly with you, right after you set up the board and alphabetize the properties." That gives you time to finish what you're doing and the child almost feels like that's part of the game.

I would like to give a high-five to all those parents who go the extra distance to balance work, children and all of the demands and pressures that come with each. This high-five is my sign of appreciation for all of the work and sacrifices you have made to make the world a better place and giving the next generation a gem, your child.

"Nothing you do for children is ever wasted. They seem not to notice us, hovering, averting our eyes, and they seldom offer thanks, but what we do for them is never wasted."
Garrison Keillor

"Children need love, especially when they don't deserve it."
Harold Hulbert

How much time can you or should you spend with your kids? Giving up your entire life for your child is counterproductive and, in fact, impossible. You can't spend every waking hour with them when they are young. As they get older, they will learn to develop their own social and work schedule. They can't depend on you for everything.

Before children are old enough to get a driver's license, their social life may be largely dependent on your willingness to cart them around. In many cases, the child can lay on some serious guilt to control the parents.

Nora's problem was a daughter who never considered her mother's needs. Nora was a a karate student whose 14-year-old daughter Leah was trying to spread her wings. She constantly nagged Nora to drive her all over the place, buy her fashionable clothes and spend time cooking for her. Leah developed a close group of friends and somehow Nora found herself living their schedule. Leah needed to be picked up from softball practice after school, to be driven to a friend's house, and then she wanted to be picked up after dinner. On other days, she needed to go to the library or a softball game. There was no end to the responsibility Nora was taking on to shadow her child's social life.

Nora was not prepared for the transition between the time a parent is in full control and the time when children start to develop their own schedule. She took her child's schedule too personally, strapping herself with an unending list of responsibilities. As she tried to balance her daughter's life and her own life, Nora was losing herself. She made it to karate class less and less and seemed more and more stressed every time she did.

When I asked how she was doing, she rattled off all of the new responsibilities she had taken on. Nora told me she needed a break and couldn't seem to detach herself from her daughter's schedule.

I suggested she contact other parents about a car-pooling system, something that might make life easier for them, too. I also told her the best technique is to sometimes just tell her daughter no. Whenever Nora did not feel up to driving around or wanted to spend time doing things she enjoyed, she had to put her foot down.

Nora found herself in that situation only two days later. She had an especially stressful day at work and wanted to recover from a daylong headache. Nora put on her slippers, made a cup of tea and sank into the recliner in the TV room when Leah came trotting in with her friend Melanie.

"Mom, we want to go to the movies," Leah said.

"I would love to take you to the movies, and I will next week when I don't have a headache."

"But mom, we made plans and really wanted to go tonight. Melanie can't go next week," Leah pleaded.

"I'm sorry to hear that. I am still not driving you to the movies."

And that was the end of it. Leah and Melanie managed to have fun hanging out in the house. Nora spent the evening in reading a book just as she envisioned and the next day she felt 100 percent better. She took Leah to the schoolyard to practice hitting for softball and the incident the night before was a distant memory. After Nora began setting limits on her time commitments to Leah, she grabbed hold of life and enjoyed her new found free time.

Leah took the bus more often than she'd like and she had to pay for it with her allowance. But she learned to live with her restrictions and worked hard so that she would be able to meet her responsibilities on her own. Mother and daughter grew from the experience.

The toughest time in a child's life may be when the unthinkable happens: mom and dad decide they don't want to be together anymore. This shatters a child's security and leads to questions about whether he or she will still have both parents' love.

Divorce is devastating for the parents and, as frequently noted, hardest on the children. Think about how divorce will hurt your child before you take that step. Make special efforts to give your child confidence that family will still be there in times of need. Both parents need to continue to say I love you more than ever.

In some cases, one parent divorces the spouse and the child. This is deplorable. The child is bound to be emotionally hurt and need an extra effort from the other parent. This unfortunate situation requires a steady hand of guidance and barrels of patience.

Sometimes love means saying no. You feel an obligation to protect your child from harm. If that means preventing your child from doing some of the things he wants to do, then so be it. Life can be dangerous and unpredictable. Saying no is a sign that you will accept your children's anger in exchange for your comfort that they are safe and for the knowledge that they are likely to be happy and healthier in the long run.

When your children misbehave, they need to experience consequences, but they always need to know that you still love them. That does not belittle the impact of the lesson. It cements the message that you are not punishing them out of anger, hate or impatience. You are doing it for their own good to teach them the difference between right and wrong.

When the going gets tough, love can be tough. Continue to say 'I love you.'

Hugs and kisses go a long way, even for macho men. The following story illustrates that fact. Dale is a 46-year-old firefighter with two sons, ages eight and thirteen. He did not give them hugs and kisses to show his love. He gave them action figures, video games and games of catch. But when he saw his nine-year-old niece Angelica, he always greeted her with big bear hugs and a kiss on the top of the head.

When Dale was young, his dad showed affection by playing fighting games and doing so-called macho things, which were never followed by hugs and kisses. Dale re-created that same relationship with his sons. This came naturally because he worked in a male-dominated field devoid of supportive hugs and kisses, and he was raised to believe this is the natural interaction between men.

This is not the case.

Male children need physical affection just as much as female children. Dale knew how to be physically expressive because he was affectionate with Angelica, but it took a very dramatic moment in Dale's life to turn the corner and allow him to show affection to his sons.

On Sept.11, 2001, more than 300 firefighters died when they raced inside two burning buildings to try to save many of the thousands of people trapped inside. The twin towers of the World Trade Center crashed down on those heroes after they had directed many people to safety.

Dale's younger brother Terry was a New York City firefighter with a company less than 30 minutes from the trade center. When the images flashed on his television screen, Dale was afraid that his brother was among the victims. He called Terry's cell phone and kept getting a busy signal. When he finally got through, he only reached Terry's voicemail. Dale reasoned that even if Terry wasn't at the trade center, he would be busy working somewhere in the city trying to help out with the tragedy and couldn't answer his phone. Dale wanted to hightail it to New York to look for him, but all roads in and out were closed.

By 10:29 a.m., the buildings had collapsed. Dale saw fire officials tell news crews about losing hundreds of men. He tried to stay strong for his children and took them to a karate class that night. Dale told his instructor the story in a panicked voice while his children ran drills on the floor. His instructor brought him into his office and talked to him for a few minutes about his efforts to reach his brother.

About seven hours had passed since the collapse and there was still no word from Terry. Dale called his mother, but she hadn't heard from Terry either. While Dale fought to keep his "strong face," his instructor offered him the only bit of comfort he thought might help. He gave him a hug.

Dale broke down. He did not cringe from the hug. Instead, he returned it. It was exactly what he needed. It was a humbling image that this strong ox of a man could be so afraid that he started tearing up. As Dale and his instructor talked, Dale recovered enough to go back out near the training floor and wait for his children to finish class. Dale was totally stressed and strung out when he came into the karate school that night. Now, even though his brother might still be in danger, he looked like a weight had been lifted from his shoulders.

At 3 o'clock the next morning, the instructor's phone rang. It was Dale. He was so happy he couldn't wait to tell him the news. It turned out that Terry wasn't on duty that day. He was in New Jersey the whole time looking for a new house. When he found out about the collapse, Terry scrambled to the scene to help pick up the pieces, leaving his phone in his jacket.

That day was an eye opener for Dale. He started to show more affection to his children. He learned to appreciate the small things and the substantial value of something as effortless as a hug. No one had to tell him hugging was a good idea. He figured it out on his own. It calmed his emotions and gave him an outlet for one of the toughest days of his life. He learned to appreciate the opportunity to hug his boys. And when he saw his brother Terry a week later, I'll bet he was met with a hearty hug, too.

He may have resented the lack of hugs when he was young, or had a hard time forming meaningful relationships with people because he didn't open up. Even though Dale was a great dad, he was continuing an unhealthy tradition that he had learned from his parents. He had just fallen into some habits he learned when he was young without fully thinking them through.

Think about what kind of parent you are. Consider what you like and dislike about how your parents raised you and whether you use some of the same methods. Take some time to review how you punish your children and consider whether it fits into your overall parenting philosophy. If not, change it immediately. Everyone will raise his or her children differently and there is no one right way. There are millions of right ways to raise your kids. Your right way depends on how closely you stick to a positive parenting attitude.

Love Thy Neighbor

"If you judge people, you have no time to love them."

Mother Theresa

It is easy to judge people who are struggling to raise their children. Show the same understanding and kindness to those people, as you would hope they'd show for you if you hit tough times. Everyone makes mistakes, including parents. Did you ever lose your temper when your teenager was more than two hours late? Were you wrong when you told your son he couldn't join his friends for basketball because you had a headache and didn't feel like dealing with it? Did you get too angry too sharp when your daughter put all the dishes in the dishwasher then forgot to turn it on? Maybe you lectured a few occasions that didn't warrant a lecture.

Working through mistakes takes time, patience, understanding and support. Offer these things to any parents you know are struggling. Criticizing people who aren't keeping up with the demands of life isn't going to make their life better. Remember, like children, they don't need to hear, "You should have..." Take the high road and reach out to someone. Helping others is its own reward. Your influence may make all the difference in whether a child is a success or succumbs to hard times. Lost children do not remain lost children. They become lost teenagers, lost adults and lost seniors dependent on society to take care of them. By stepping in and making efforts to help other families, you are making the future brighter and handing children a better society to take over.

Love for a child is like a candle flame. Even in the dark, the light is visible. Let your love be that flame through the sadness and disappointment in life. That tiny light may be all the child needs to see through to the other side of the darkness. Keep that flame burning in the best of times and worst of times.

Even when your children are doing things you don't like, respect them and love them. When your daughter wears too much lipstick and your son gets a nose ring, continue to show that you love who they are.

"Don't throw away your friendship with your teenager over behavior that has no great moral significance. There will be plenty of real issues that require you to stand like a rock. Save your big guns for those crucial confrontations."

Dr. James C. Dobson

Chapter 11

Be A Role Model And Set A Good Example

"I'm not a teacher, but an awakener."
Robert Frost

Don't be a hypocrite.

Practice what you preach.

Do unto others as you'd have them do unto you.

There are many ways to say "Be a role model," but only one way to do it. Take Action.

It's important to want to be a good parent, but it's also important to have the skills to be a good role model.

The Moral Question

How well you decide to raise your children is entirely dependent on your morals, values, ideology and largely how you were raised. Black Belt Parenting is a guide to help fill in the blanks when there is no answer in your own value system. My intention is that this book helps you build on your natural parenting skills. It was written to give you small actions you can take to enhance those skills, offering concrete recommendations and help you guide your children in the right direction. Your children are important. Every advantage you have in raising them will make your life and their lives easier.

This book is not an effort to replace your morals or to dictate them. If you have a different strategy for teaching your child consequences to his or her actions, that is okay. It is important that you recognize various options and come up with a reasonable justification for the option you choose. Will it make your child a better person? Will it teach them a lesson? Does the punishment fit the crime? If you answer yes to all three questions, you have adequately thought through your actions and you are making a logical decision on how to raise your child. It is up to you to decide where there is room for improvement in your parenting style.

What unites every person reading this book and every person who has children is that we all want what is best for our children (no matter how many times we have to remind them of that.) We want them to be respectful, goal-oriented, forward thinking, compassionate, strong and happy. In the process, though, we must have those attributes to show children how it is done.

Above all, the most effective way to teach values and morals to your children is to consistently live them. If that means following an organized religious doctrine for instance, do so faithfully. Follow the religious principles, attend services regularly and search for guidance through the institution.

If one of your values is prioritizing relaxation over money, do so faithfully. Do not lose sight of this, no matter how tempting it may be. A common excuse of workaholics is the need for money. Nowhere is this more apparent than among the wealthiest people.

Money Isn't Time

The Bradford children take karate twice a week and live in one of the largest houses in the county. Maribelle, 7, and Frankie, 14, attend an exclusive private school and can afford all of the luxuries in life, including new karate uniforms and any other accessories they wish for. Each child comes to class wearing his or her choice of uniforms, decorated with several patches, and carrying top-of-the-line training weapons. The only thing missing is their father.

Franklin Bradford is a workaholic managing a stock-trading group. He rarely comes into the school to see his children perform in their designer uniforms. He rarely spends time with them at all, except to write out checks. Maribelle and Frankie are spoiled, yes, but they are also good kids. And they miss their father. When Frankie earned his Black Belt, Mr. Bradford came to the awards ceremony and I invited him to join us in class more often. He said that he didn't have time because of his work.

On one hand, I sympathize with the need to work really hard to keep a good-paying job. On the other, I realize that a good-paying job isn't worth much if you can't enjoy time with your children. If I were to ask Mr. Bradford what is more important to him, I'm sure he would say his children. He certainly tried hard

Black Belt Parenting

to compensate for not being there by buying them things. He wanted them to be happy.

The disconnect lies in his behavior. He wants the best for his children, but he fails to see what is the most valuable asset for any child: time with mom and dad. He may say that money is not as important as his children, but he isn't showing it. What lesson does that teach his children? First, that money is a priority. Second, that it is okay to say one thing and do another. The children are getting mixed messages. Being a role model means being consistent with your message.

The best thing for the children is for Mr. Bradford to sit down with them and have a long talk about the value of money. He would be well served to hold onto his wallet and hold out his hand to hug his children, toss them a ball or walk them to the ice-cream store. Frankie is at an age when he is getting ready to start dating girls and take responsibility for himself. He needs someone around who can offer him more than a green piece of paper.

Whatever your morals, stick to them.

Whatever your parenting strategy, don't sacrifice it just so your child will be your friend. Take time to play with your children. No matter how responsible and respected you are in your daily life, you have a free pass to drop all of that professionalism and perfectionism when you are with your child. The best way to reach children and bring them to your level is to first go down to theirs. Deep down you have the sensibilities of a child. You have the desire to play and laugh all day. Inside you is a person who wants to play peek-a-boo, or catch or hide and seek. Let go of your inhibitions and let your playful side out. Go beyond the role of and look at life from a kid's level.

Teenagers may not want a mom who critiques pop stars and talks on the phone all day like they do. Sometimes, though, you can be laid back about the music they listen to or clothes they wear to relate on their level. Don't let the generational gap stand in the way.

Age and experience separate you. Find something - anything- to help you connect. They may not be enlightened by a "When I was your age" story. They were not around in the world you grew up in and are unlikely to relate to it. Look for something in their world. Maybe you like some of the same movies, TV shows, music or books. Talk about those things and invite the teen to join you at the theatre, watching the tube or on a trip to the bookstore. Remember that you are a parent, not a friend. Just because you like a movie, that doesn't mean it is appropriate for your children. Don't feel obligated to let them join you in whatever they want. You make the rules. Every parent draws the line in a different place. Teaching children lessons about life and setting a good example may take an amazing amount of endurance and strength.

Understanding, Not Blame

"You have no control over what the other guy does. You only have control over what you do."

A. J. Kitt

Don't play the blame game, even if you're right. I get so disappointed when I see good parents resorting to the blame game whenever they or their child faces an obstacle. It is common when there are problems in a school district or sports. If Timmy loses in a baseball game, don't blame it on a referee's bad call, simply say, "You played a great game."

In the past few years, there has been a spate of violence and corruption in childrens sporting events – and it isn't among the tikes on the field. It's the "role models" out in the stands who are wreaking havoc, making fools of themselves and embarrassing their children. In sports games, parents frequently fight with each other or cuss out the coach or refs if the game isn't going as well as they would like. Sometimes your child might not get as much playing time as you would like. Sometimes a ref makes a bad call. Other times another player gets away with a penalty against your child. Yelling, screaming and fighting will not solve the problem. Remember, no one can take away your child's talent. As long as he or she works hard, their abilities will show on the playing field, in spite of a few questionable calls. In the game of life, there is a lot of room for human error.

Refrain from blaming others – even if you believe they are culpable. Blaming others sends the message that you are trying to deflect responsibility. Think about what you can do to make the situation better. This is not about out lasting someone in an argument, getting in the last word, or proving you are right. We are talking about being good role models for children.

It is no secret that your children will face obstacles in which they won't have the opportunity to blame someone else, even if it's not their fault. For example, if Damon works all night on a homework assignment and the computer crashes, he faces a serious challenge. And thought it's not his fault, he still has to figure out how to get the work done. He can't call the school and complain that the assignment put too much of a burden on him. He can't call the computer company and force them to recover his lost work. Damon has seen his parents blame a referee's "bad call" for his own error on the ball field and he thinks about following their example. Instead of solving the problem, he starts thinking "How can I blame this on someone or some thing else?"

When Damon enters the work force, his boss may ask him to do things that he can't get done. He can blame others all he wants, but the boss won't want to hear it. He wants to hear what Damon is going to do to fix the problem. And you want to teach Damon, by your own behavior, how to take a situation you can't control and improve it. Teach him that when things don't go his way, he has to brainstorm to compensate for unavoidable accidents or the mistakes of others. He has to try to make the situation better for all involved.

When a 13-year-old boy took scissors during arts and crafts and cut off another girl's hair he was suspended. How would you expect his mother to react? Anger at the child? Happy that the school prevented him from accidentally hurting someone or himself? No, the mother in this case blamed the school! She said the teachers shouldn't have given him scissors in the first place. "Students shouldn't have access to scissors if the teachers aren't watching them. I don't trust the school. How do I know this kind of thing won't happen again?"

I agree that children should be reasonably supervised in school, but there was no way a teacher could have been vigilant enough to prevent that prank. If the teacher had kept a close enough watch on the 13-year-old, the rest of the class would have been relatively unsupervised. That boy was old enough to know better and he made a poor decision. His mother needed to take responsibility to punish her child. Her son needed to take responsibility for what he did. When she made excuses, she did demonstrative harm in that he thinks he didn't do anything wrong. If she didn't teach him right from wrong, he will continue the cycle of making excuses and will never learn one of life's most important lessons – take responsibility for your own actions.

Keeping children in line is increasingly difficult as they age. The older a child is, the less likely he or she is to learn from your mistakes. As you will read in the upcoming story, three-year-old Jen learned that stealing is wrong after she and her mother were punished at the supermarket. A 14-year-old won't be so quick to learn a lesson. Any mistake you make that is counter to your message is like kicking a pit bull. The child will latch onto that flaw and won't let go. The jaws of childhood stubbornness will dig into your hypocrisy and a 14-year-old has stronger jaws than a young child. Don't give the child an opportunity to bite.

"There is nothing so annoying as a good example."
Mark Twain

No Smoking And Nonpareils

A common example of a parent's actions not matching words is smoking. Children who see their parents smoke insist that it's okay. Remember, it's not what you say. It's what you do. If the child sees the parent who smokes as happy, healthy and loving, the connection between smoking and disease will never be made. In this case there are two choices: (1) be miserable, angry and depressed to connect smoking with sickness or (2) quit smoking.

Don't waver about what you want a young child to do. Be clear with your messages. If you tell them that hitting is wrong, don't give them any exceptions, especially when they are too young to understand. This is why our youngest students are not permitted to spar. They have to become accustomed to the system and recognize the difference between class and real life

152   *Black Belt Parenting*

before we arm them with that ability. There may be times when you have to hit to defend yourself or to stop someone else from being seriously harmed by another. But this is beyond a young child's comprehension.

"You have to set the tone and the pace, define objectives and strategies, demonstrate through personal example what you expect from others."

Stanley C. Gault

When Jen was three, she frequently accompanied her mother to the supermarket. She liked to push the cart and pick out a few items that mom wouldn't have bought on her own, especially treats out of the candy bin. While filling a small bag of nonpareils for Jen, mom popped a few into her mouth. Being the astute child that she is, Jen noticed that her mom did not pay for those two or three items. She took that as her cue to eat whatever she wanted before getting to the checkout line. After all, if mom didn't pay for those, she didn't have to buy the dozen or so in Jen's baggie. So when mom wasn't looking, Jen discretely put the bag of candy in her coat pocket and slipped them into her mouth one at a time. When mom got to the checkout line, she didn't even realize the nonpareils weren't in the cart. Jen didn't complain about it when they got home, so it didn't even cross mom's mind that something was missing. With the candy out of sight, she didn't even think about what might have happened to it.

Two days later mom was trying to pull Jen's gloves out of the pocket and she found the baggy with a few sprinkles at the bottom. She was angry. She confronted Jen and was shocked to hear her response.

"Jen, you ate this candy without paying for it!" she said.

"But mommy you did it," Jen said.

"What? No I didn't."

"But I saw you. You ate some when you were filling my bag."

"But I only ate a couple," Mom responded.

"So did I," Jen said. "I ate one at a time, too."

Jen was right. There was no way to explain the difference in scope of stealing one nonpareil as opposed to a dozen. She shouldn't have set the precedent that it was okay to eat anything before it's paid for. She realized her mistake and decided to do something to set Jen straight. She would have to incriminate herself in the process.

At the risk of her own embarrassment, she carted Jen to the customer service line at the supermarket and asked to see the supervisor. She explained what happened and said she wanted to teach her daughter a lesson. The manager appreciated the effort and agreed that Jen and her mom should be punished. He charged them for an entire pound of nonpareils since he had no way of measuring how much they ate. Plus, he said they were not allowed to buy candy at the supermarket for the next two months. Jen learned her lesson and mom will think twice about the example she sets. Jen's mom got a good lesson in how closely her actions will be replicated by her child.

Keep your word to your children. Credibility is very important. They remember everything you say and especially everything you don't say. Children will remember what you do and how you acted and they will not let you get away with it.

The ability of a child will always be one step below that of the parent, just as a team is only as strong as its weakest link. If your ability to lead is a three, under your wing the child will struggle to be a two. Whoever you lead will always be one step behind you. If you don't raise the bar on yourself, you won't be pushing them to their limits. Eventually they catch up to you and hopefully surpass you. If you are a good leader, you will create good leaders. When the bulk of your responsibility ends and the horserace is on, there will be no question as to whether your child will be leading the pack.

Measure Your Skills

Try this exercise to measure your ability and desire as a parent. Draw the vertical and horizontal lines of a grid, like a giant L. Label the vertical side "parenting leadership ability." Label the horizontal side "desire to be a great parent." Where would you rate yourself right now in desire and ability? Most parents when faced with this challenge will plot a point far out on the grid when it comes to desire. As for ability, the number could be a one or two. Even though the desire has reached its limit, ability needs to be nurtured.

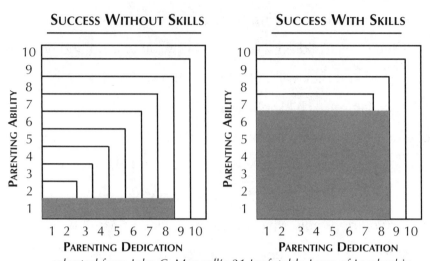

Talking about parenting may motivate some people to think about it more and be more excited about their desire. Some parents want to learn everything there is to know about the subject. The overall consensus is that parents have an immense desire to fulfill that role well. The question is: What are they doing to improve their ability.

Leaps and bounds of progress are possible if parents are willing to make the commitment. Improvement on the desire scale is measured in tiny increments. On the ability scale, there is more room for improvement to completely meet potential.

Raise The Bar

Do more than you are expected to do.

Encourage your children to do more than is required. Allow them to be overachievers by challenging them to do more than they think they can. I apply this teaching method in class. When it is time to do push-ups, I assign the class 10, but implore the overachievers to do 15. I say that the strongest kids—and they should know who they are—should do 15. Most children will strive for 15. They want to be in that category. And by going that extra step, they are the strongest kids in class. They have the strongest will and desire.

Sweat It Out

Turn negatives into positives. Most people don't like to sweat, even children. If they work too hard in class and break a sweat, some will stop trying because they feel uncomfortable. When a guest instructor was at the school, he was pumped up and wanted to leave a good impression on the class. The advanced class was impressed with his skills and labored to keep up. When 14-year-old Nathan was trembling as he tried to straighten his elbow for one last push-up, the guest instructor wiped his fingers across Nathan's forehead and asked, "What's this?"

When Nathan dropped to the ground after his push-up, he half-smiled and answered,

"It's sweat."

"No it's not," he countered. "It's progress!"

All of a sudden the sweat wasn't so hot and sticky. It became a symbol of accomplishment. The more you sweat in a workout, the harder you work.

Always Take This Advice

Don't be overly dramatic in your praise or punishment. Don't exaggerate the scope of a problem using words like "everybody" "always" and "never." It sounds ridiculous when children do it and it is just as ridiculous when adults do it.

Some examples are:

"You never do your chores on time."

"You are always on the phone."

"Everybody's doing it."

"I'm the only person in the world who has to deal with this mess."

Dramatic generalizations belabor the point far beyond what is necessary. The child does the chores on time sometimes, right? Is the phone really in use 24 hours a day? And you're never the only one. The problems of raising children are universal.

In the way it is explained to you, you child's version of daily life will be vastly different from what daily life is actually like. Things that all the other kids are doing are most likely: (1) things some of the child's friends wants to be doing or (2) things a select few of the child's friends are doing, most likely because their parents think the other kids are doing it or because they are not actively engaged in the child's life.

Being a role model is a full-time job. When you fall down on that job, learn from your misstep and don't let it happen again.

Be a good role model. Set a good example. Be a Black Belt Parent.

Chapter 12

Fueling Up With: High Octane

*Written Especially
For Black Belt Parenting
By Dave Weist*

This chapter will touch on some of the ways we can help our children cope with the ever-growing stress of life. As our children grow, they learn the ways of the world. Our society puts so much pressure on our kids it is to some degree a shame. *Let your kids be kids.* Let them enjoy the child within and let them play. They have the rest of their lives to be adults.

Playing is one of the most important aspects of a child's life and is probably the best learning experience he or she will ever have. Children learn 80% of all they learn in life by age five. Your children rely on you to make wise choices for shaping their future and guiding them down the right road. It is an unbelievable responsibility to raise children, especially in this high speed country we live in. The pressure is astounding. Kids are learning things in the fifth grade many of today's adults didn't learn until high school. We are bombarding our children with sports and other after-school activities and some kids have tons of homework plus all of the other daily chores and duties of life.

Parents must incorporate two words into their <u>Black Belt Parenting</u> vocabulary: *moderation* and *responsibility.* First, we must make certain our children are eating the best possible foods for their proper physical and mental development. Second, we must understand that moderation is the key to a favorable and healthy diet. Diet is not used here in reference to weight loss, but in the sense of a daily program of eating and drinking proper foods. If parents do not take the responsibility to make sure their children are eating right, I can guarantee you they will think a "balanced breakfast" means a soda, two cream filled donuts and a candy bar.

As your children grow, train them as to what is good and what is not good to eat. These days their taste senses are being trained to love only sweets. Soon they will have been trained to like only the sweetest and most colorful foods. But they can also be trained to like the real foods that Mother Nature put here. They can learn to love the taste of fresh fruit and how awesome that treat is for the human body. They can learn to avoid the artificially sweetened, processed, colored, dyed and preserved foods that are so common in today's society.

As society has changed and we have gone from a one- to two-income families, it is even harder to help our kids with life events. Children are much more independent and much more self sufficient then they used to be. We all need to drive the big fancy car and have the surround sound and the cell phone, but at what expense? Are we better off having more independent children or should we try to keep them children until they decide to turn into young adults? What can we, as parents, do to help and guide our children through life, not only when they are children but as adults? With the proper guidance of a parent and other great role models, our children will make excellent parents.

Children are a factory of ever growing and ever changing cells. These cells, whether cells of the brain, heart, arms, legs or toes multiply at an extraordinary rate. To do this, they need energy and that energy comes in the form of food.

Food the cells need to survive must be from the best source possible. Many food companies add colors and dyes to foods to make them appear more appealing and to attract us into buying them. They especially use the ingredients in the foods targeted to our children.

We have more than sugar to worry about. Many of today's foods are loaded with food coloring and dyes. There is a publication in the federal government known as publication 96-252 and it prohibits the Federal Trade Commission (FTC) from enacting rules that would protect our kids from being exploited by advertisers. What is wrong with these added colors and dyes? They reflect light at a specific wavelength. These wavelengths can interact with the DNA in our bodies and cause cancer. Many colors and dyes have been pulled from the safe list because they have been found to cause cancer or other degenerative diseases. This is another reason to make sure that your children are eating only the best foods.

Another subject we need to ponder is what happens to these artificial ingredients when we heat them through cooking. These are for the most part chemical compounds that have been created in a laboratory. Most chemicals when heated change their molecular state. What state are they changing to and what will that altered state do to our bodies?

Think about your car for a moment, if you put regular gas in a car that needs premium you're going to get substandard performance. If you put premium fuel in that same car you'll get premium performance. Kids are the race cars of society. How many times have you said, "If I only had a quarter of that kid's energy?" Where does this energy come from? It comes form the fuels that you put in their gas tank. These fuels have to be of the highest quality and they have to be all natural. The human body is all natural, nothing fake. The foods the all-natural body has to have must also be all natural. Kids need the real thing to sustain their bodies so they can perform like the miracles they are.

We all know that without food we can't survive. Without water our survival is in even more jeopardy. Water makes up about 90 percent of our blood. It helps the blood to flow as well as keeping the kidneys clean and the liver functioning as designed. When you feel thirsty, it is already too late. Your body is giving you a warning sign that you need to drink. At this point, you have already started to dehydrate. It is essential that we take in enough water to assure proper functioning of our bodily systems. Six to eight glasses a day is about right for the average human.

Food is the energy our bodies need to run. Good food is the energy our bodies need to run right. As we learn more and more about proper eating habits it is so evident that we as a society do not eat right. In America, children and teenagers drink about 54 billion dollars worth of soft drinks a year. That's about 14 million gallons per year and about 868 cans per kid per year. This is staggering. Do you think the soft drink industry is interested in your child's health or are they interested in profits? The soft drink and junk food industries target children. All they are interested in is getting us to drink more and to train our kids to spend a life time of eating and drinking their sugary products. Here's another statistic that will floor you: 25% to 30% of our children are clinically obese in this country.

We need to supervise our children's lives and that includes what they eat. This is one of the most important aspects of their growth. Reading the ever growing list of attention deficit syndromes that our children have is scary. Why is this list on what seems to be a continual growth pattern? Take the time to look and understand what our children are eating in this country and you will begin to understand why we have labels such as ADD and ADHD. These two conditions have been overdiagnosed. Why are so many children being labeled with this acronym? Look at the foods we are letting our children consume. Remember, the major food companies are most interested in profits.

We have a responsibility to teach our children what is right and wrong. As our children are being fed this sugar-laced junk food, they are being trained that this is the way to eat. Sugar in that form creates a quick high, but after the high a depression sets in. First, the sugars that are used in soft drinks and candy are horrible for us to consume. Cane sugar is taken to the factory and run through a press. This press squeezes out all of the water and juice. After it is pressed, it is then bleached so it looks pretty and white. Next, all of the nutrients are taken out and finally it is crystallized. This is total garbage.

As our children consume fake cereals with all of that sugar, they get an instant high. About an hour later they start to come off of this high and are mentally and physically doomed. As their bodies realize that they are starved for energy, they look for food. Now comes the worst part. They have been trained to look for the high-sugar processed foods, the quick fix, the sugar rush. The roller coaster ride begins goes on all day until finally at night they crash and go to bed.

The average American eats about 63 pounds of candy a year. That's the average American, including adults. Children I am sure are much higher. In 1999, we spent more on sugar, about 158 pounds per person, than in the history of the country and we wonder why our kids are so hyperactive. A 1995 study found that sugar taken on an empty stomach led to an inability to concentrate.

There is an alternative: fruit. Fruit with all of its natural sugars takes a little more time to affect the energy level but once it does, it is there to stay for quite a long period of time. As they go throughout the day eating properly and understanding what is and is not good for them, their bodies become regulated. We can train our taste buds to like any kind of food. It is time to train them to like real good, tasty, quality natural foods.

Parents must take the initiative to understand and become aware of what is out there in the food market and what is and is not good for both themselves and their children. Remember that the food industry does not care and neither does the Federal Government.

Get a box of your children's favorite cereal and read the ingredients. First thing on the list or one of the first things will be sugar. Next, you'll see one or two or maybe even three of the FD&C dyes or colors, many of which are known to cause degenerative diseases. What else is on that list? Probably some kind of preservative and I am sure one of the hydrogenated oils. All of the hydrogenated oils are bad for you. The human body does not recognize these oils, colors, dyes and preservatives.

Now let's go back and think about why our children are so hyperactive. Does anyone really know at this point what these fake ingredients are doing to us? Fortunately there are groups out there starting to study the problem. They are finding that these things are not good for us.

As the food industry continues to try and sell us on their goods, they must become ever more creative. Green ketchup? Purple ketchup? Come on, give me a break. What are they trying to do? Can ketchup sales be that bad? Another company now makes pink and blue butter to try and boost their sales. I guess the competition in the butter industry is really tough. Profits are the underlying drive of these companies. The problem is similar to that with the soft drink companies. We do not fully understand what these colors and dyes are doing to us. A child's body is constantly growing and using the foods that he or she eats to build the cells that make the body. All of these foreign substances being introduced makes it hard to believe that the body can do its job. What are these laboratory foods doing to our children?

Let's talk a little about the lunch program. There has been much pressure put on the school system to provide lunch and even breakfast for our children. Kids are going to school hungry because we don't have the time to make them a good breakfast. Breakfast is the time of day when you *break the fast* you have been on while asleep. It is the most important meal of the day, especially for children. A child's body is a fuel guzzling engine that must have complete nourishment.

Take a good look at the foods that are being served at our schools and you will be amazed. The food—and I use that term loosely—at our schools is disgusting. No wonder the kids are sitting there like they have ants in their pants. Once again it comes back to us, the parents, who are ultimately responsible for our children's nourishment.

What can we do to help our children to calm down, sleep better and have the energy to make it through a school day without falling asleep, failing subjects, wearing out in gym class and having to take drugs to control hyperactivity? To begin we must make sure that they get enough sleep. That's essential. You and especially your children should be getting at least eight hours of sleep a night. Children frequently tell me about the television programs they watched the previous night. Often, these shows were not even suitable for a child to be watching and were on much too late.

Why do we have to sleep? This is one of the many mysteries of the world, but we do know that without it you die. Sleep is when the brain refuels. Sleep helps growth and development, conserves energy, lowers the brain temperature, enhances memory and enhances the immune system. Proper sleep and proper nutrition will make the time at school much easier for your children.

Here are some startling statistics about what our kids are and are not eating. Only 34% of boys and 33% of girls are eating the recommended amount of vegetables. That leaves the rest, 66% of boys and 67% of girls, not eating the recommended amount. Only 11% of boys and 16% of girls are eating the recommended amount of fruit. That leaves 89% of boys and 84% of girls deficient in fruit intake. Most kids are not eating the recommended amount of grains and protein. Clearly, the vast majority of our children are not eating properly.

There is something else to consider when we are talking about food and the ingredients that are in the foods we are eating. Let's take a look at some of the additives that are put into our foods to make them look nicer and more colorful, and look at some of the adverse effects that some of these dyes and colors have on the human body.

Color/Dye	Effect
FD&C Red No. 40	Tumors / Lymphomas
Citrus Red No. 2	Cancer in animals
FD&C Blue No. 2	Brain tumors
	Bronchonstriction
FD&C Yellow No. 6	Kidney tumors
	Brain tumors

FD&C Yellow No. 6 (cont'd)	Allergies
	Vomiting
	Indigestion
	Distaste for food
	And eight other
	adverse effects

These statistics are astounding and we, as the parenting force of this country, should be ashamed of the diets our children are eating. Not only have these chemicals been linked to some of the most degenerative diseases in the world, they have been under scrutiny for possibly having some effect with neurotransmitters of the brain. This may possibly have some effect on concentration and behavioral changes especially in children.

There are so many easy and delicious foods we can make for breakfast and many foods that we can send with our children for lunch. Let's start with breakfast. First, commit to quality and get only the best quality foods. We want foods with no preservatives, artificial colors and dyes and no foods with hydrogenated oils. We want whole grains, natural sugars, and plenty of fruit. Remember fruit contains the natural sugars to give them the energy to make it through the day.

In the morning there are many different kinds of frozen waffles that you can just pop in the toaster. After they are done, add some good berries and maple syrup. Cereal is another great breakfast item. Again, remember what ingredients should and shouldn't be in the cereal. Add some fruit like raisins, blue berries, bananas, raspberries, almost any kind of fruit that you can think of. Use skim milk or better yet some of the soy or rice milks that are on the market and again you can feel good about sending them to school.

What else makes a good breakfast? Another fast and easy idea is whole wheat toast with preserves and a glass of orange juice. Whatever your choices are, make sure they include at least one or more type of fruit. If you take a minute to think about it, you will be able to give them the fuel they need to get them started and to run until lunch.

Lunch is probably one of the most difficult meals to make. First, you have to make something that is portable and that will last a few hours. The old staple of peanut butter and jelly is always a good idea, but make sure that the peanut butter is 100% natural. Many of the major brands have a lot of sugar and hydrogenated oils. Make sure the preserves are all natural with no artificial colors or dyes. Smooth it on good, high-quality bread for an excellent source of energy to carry them through the rest of the day. As an alternative, you can always use almond butter instead of peanut butter. You can make this sandwich in about a thousand varieties.

There are many wholesome prepared lunches, but you have to read the labels. Be wary. Many of these prepared foods marketed to our children are fit for neither man nor beast.

Whatever you send, make sure to add some fruit. If you need to send a drink, then there are many great drinks that are all natural and without all of the sugars regular sodas and fake fruit juices contain. Some soy and rice drinks are awesome. They taste great, are very nutritious and come in different flavors. There are also natural sodas free of chemicals or preservatives. These drinks will help your child to make it through the rest of the day without any sugar rushes or any down time after the sugar rush. Proper nutrition fuels the body and brain for hours.

There is no healthy substitute for good quality, nutritious food. There is also no emotional substitute for sitting down and having a great healthy meal with the family. This serves not only as a great way to introduce children to good foods, but also to learn what's going on in their lives. Involvement is the key to having your child grow up to be the wonderful person that he or she can be. A child is a precious gift to all parents and the best gift you will ever have. Take the time to nourish body and soul to the best of your ability and you will get nothing in return but love from your child. Remember, to be a parent and not a friend. The lessons you teach, for good or ill, will be carried on for generations.

Why not practice Black Belt Parenting and know that what you teach will be having a positive influence for generations to come?

www.thenutritiontree.com
(215) 357-1952

ORDER FORM

For Mail Orders, send **Check** (payable to Action Karate) or completed **Credit Card** Information to:

Action Karate
1824 Bridgetown Pike
Feasterville, PA 19053

Quantity_____ @ $19.95 ea. + shipping (3.95ea.) = _____

Credit Card (circle one)   VISA   MasterCard   DISCOVER

Card Number _____

Expiration Date _____

Name on Card _____

Telephone _____

SHIP TO:

Name _____

Organization/Company _____

Address _____

City/State/ZIP _____

Telephone _____